The Gifted Woman

A Look at Spiritual Gifts

by
Patricia L. Welch

The Gifted Woman

A Look at Spiritual Gifts

2013

Welch Publishing ISBN:978-0-578-13382-9

Printed in the United States of America

Table of Contents

Acknowledgements

I thank God for opening my eyes to my motivational gift, and for giving me opportunity to teach this course on Spiritual Gifts to thousands of women over the years to help them find their gift and purpose in life.

I also want to thank the following people for their invaluable help as I studied, taught, and now publish this book on The Gifted Woman.

First and foremost, I want to thank <u>Bill Gothard's Institute.</u> <u>of Basic Life Principles</u> for giving me permission to use their material to address women. Bill Gothard was such a help to my own spiritual growth during the early years of my Christian walk, and I consider it an honor to be able to use and teach this material.

Secondly, I want to thank all the women who were willing to write out their Spiritual gift testimony to be included in this book so that others could get a visual picture of how God can use each gift in ordinary lives.

And then I want to thank the ladies in "Women of Gace" life group who agreed to go through this book with me so I could fine-tune it for publication.

And, of course, my husband, Francis Welch, who faithfully reads over my work and makes helpful suggestions. Not to mention his patience as I study, write, and rewrite. ♥

Introduction

Discovering your spiritual gift will be one of the most exciting and joyful moments in your Christian life. Many Christians sit in church on Sunday, but have no idea what their purpose is in the plan of God. Discovering your spiritual gift will help you find that purpose.

By the end of this study you will probably understand yourself better than you ever have before, and at the same time understand others also.

We will discover what spiritual gifts are, what they are not, how to develop them, and how to exercise them. We will see specific characteristics of each gift.

Our main text will be the motivational gifts of Romans 12, although we will touch briefly on other passages as well.

If you're ready, let's start our journey together.

Why Focus on Spiritual Gifts?

So that we will be _informed_ - God wants us to know what our gifts are.

> *"Now concerning spiritual gifts, brethren,*
> *I would not have you ignorant."*
> I Corinthians 12:1

They are mentioned in the _Word of God_ - therefore they are important.

> *"All Scripture is given by inspiration of God*
> *and is profitable . . ."*
> II Timothy 3:16,17

We should not _neglect_ our gift - God wants us to unwrap it and put it to use.

> *"Neglect not the gift that is in you"*
> I Timothy 4:14

We are to _stir up_ our gift - Don't let it just sit there; develop and exercise it.

> *"Wherefore, I put you in remembrance that*
> *you stir up the gift of God which is in you."*
> II Timothy 1:6

We are to be _good stewards_ of our gift, _ministering to one another_ - Spiritual gifts are not given for our own self-gratification, but rather that we use them to serve others!

> *"As every man has received the gift, even so*
> *minister the same one to another, as good*
> *stewards of the manifold grace of God."*
> I Peter 4:10

Our _works_ will be _judged_ - We will each stand before God and give an account for everything He has given to us to use for His glory, including spiritual gifts.

> _"For we must all appear before the Judgment Seat_
> _of Christ, that everyone may receive the things_
> _done in his body, according to that he has done,_
> _whether it be good or bad."_
> II Corinthians 5:10

Our spiritual gift needs to be _discovered, developed,_ and _exercised._ God gave them to us for a purpose.

Definition of a spiritual gift:

Special _abilities_ that God gives His children to _accomplish_ His work. The _Holy Spirit_ gives spiritual _power_ so you can minister _to_ and _through_ the church.

A spiritual gift involves:

Motivation - the desire and power to concentrate on a particular aspect of Christian ministry.

Ability - to do an effective job.

Strength - to get the job done with a minimum of weariness

Responsibility - to use the gift God has entrusted to you

There are basically two kinds (types) of spiritual gifts according to I Peter 4:10,11:

Speaking and _Serving_

When you understand your spiritual gift, it:

Provides *personal identity*

> You won't waste your time thinking "Who am I? Why
> am I here? What does God have in mind for me?
> Where am I going?" God says you are a gifted
> person with a divine ministry on earth. You
> have a purpose.

Gives *freedom* from *false guilt*

> Once you understand that God has gifted you in a
> certain area, and you fail where He hasn't gifted you,
> you have no reason for guilt. For instance maybe
> you try teaching a life group and it just doesn't seem
> to be your thing. There is no need to feel inferior or
> guilty - you just have to try another area of service.
> Maybe God didn't create you to be a teacher, but
> wants you to be a server.

It eliminates the need for *competition* by helping you to *accept yourself* in your God-given uniqueness.

> If you know your gift is serving, you will not feel
> unworthy because you don't have the gift of
> prophecy. You have a special endowment from
> the Lord that suits you perfectly.

> The woman who knows her gift is administration
> (ruling), and is functioning effectively in that capacity,
> will not think of herself as unworthy or unnecessary
> because she is not a teacher.

> You will be accomplishing what God has equipped
> you to do, instead of comparing yourself to and
> competing with others.There is always room for a
> gifted person.

> *"A man's gift makes room for him and
> brings him before great men."* Proverbs 18:16

It can direct you into *God's* specific *will* for *your life* .

> It makes sense that if God has gifted you in a certain area, and opportunities come along for you to exercise your gift in that area, more than likely that is what God wants you to do.

It will help you set *priorities* in your life.

> If you know you are gifted as a teacher, you will never be content to be in charge of every church activity that is planned.

It will allow you to identify an area for spiritual *training* and *development*.

> The person with the gift of exhortation or mercy might want to take some counselling courses. The teacher could develop and improve her teaching by attending seminars, special classes and training workshops, learning creative teaching methods.
>
> No matter what gift you have, you can benefit from taking classes, reading, going to conferences, taking college courses, listening to DVD's, starting a resource file, subscribing to magazines, etc.
>
> We should be continually developing and fine-tuning our spiritual gift.

It will bring you *joy* and *fulfillment*.

> When you discover your gift and place of ministry, you will have great joy in your heart and a sense of fulfillment. Your attitude will be "This is what I'd rather be doing for the Lord than anything else in the world. This is my purpose. This is what gets me excited." And this enthusiasm will be subconsciously communicated to the people you minister to.

What A Spiritual Gift Is Not

It is not a *natural talent* or *ability*

> Talents are a *common* grace of God. A natural ability present from our physical birth to benefit mankind on the natural level. These talents must be recognized, developed and exercised.

> Spiritual gifts are a *special* grace of God present from our new birth in Christ to benefit mankind on the spiritual level. These gifts must be recognized, developed and exercised.

> *Balance*: *We need to dedicate our natural talents and abilities, and our spiritual gifts to the Lord to be used for His glory.*

It is not the *Fruit of the Spirit*

> Spiritual gifts have to do with service (speaking, serving). The fruit of the Spirit denotes our character (love, joy, peace, etc.) It's what is inside us.

> Gifts are what a person has, and do not always indicate godliness of life. The fruit of the Spirit shows what a person is and is proof of godliness.

> Gifts are given from without. Fruit is produced from within.

> *All* the gifts are not possessed by every believer, but *every* variety of fruit should be produced in the life of every believer.

> The gifts will cease some day, but the fruit of the Spirit is permanent (I Corinthians 13:8-10)

> *Balance*: *it is better to be godly than gifted, but better still to be godly and gifted*

It is not our _ministry_

Ministry is the vehicle through which our gift is channeled. Our spiritual gift is the empowerment for which our ministry is made effective.

Ministry is where God places us for service. Our spiritual gift is the motivation God gives us for all of our service for Him.

Our ministry may change, but our motivational spiritual gift never changes.

Balance: _We can use our gift in whatever position God places us in. When He closes one door, He'll open another._

Discovery of your gift will take:

Faith

You must believe you are gifted. God's Word teaches that each believer has a spiritual gift. Do you have faith enough to believe that and to act upon that belief?

Prayer

You need to pray for understanding. James 4:2 says "You have not because you ask not." Ask God to help you discover your gift.

Awareness

Be aware of what gifts are available and study the gifts and their characteristics. You must be informed about spiritual gifts if you hope to recognize your own.

Common Sense

This involves:
Your motivation - Why you do the things you do? What motivates you?

Your desires - What do you enjoy doing?

Your abilities - What do you do well?

Some have a picture of God's will for their lives as something they will hate. Yet Romans 12:2 tells us that the will of God is good, it is perfect and it is acceptable. It is the best thing possible and it will be uniquely blended with our gifts, talents, abilities and desires. We will be joyful in the center of God's will.

Involvement

Take advantage of opportunities that come your way and get involved in some kind of ministry. God will show you what you're good at and what you're not so good at.

Try teaching a life group. Work in the nursery. Join a mother/daughter banquet committee. Visit nursing homes. Volunteer at church during the week. Be a part of vacation Bible school. Be willing to try something new. In this way you will find out what really brings you satisfaction and joy.

Confirmation

Your gift will be confirmed in two ways:

Seeing *growth* in the lives of others because you are exercising your gift.

Other people will *verbally confirm* your gift as they recognize God working through you while you use it. At some point, mature Christians will tell you what your gift is.

God wants you to discover your gift. And you will if you begin with faith, pray, learn the characteristics of the gifts, use your common sense, and get involved.

*The key to discovering your
Motivational gift is to ask
What is my motivation for doing this?
For feeling this way?
For behaving in this manner?*

Every gift, as we will discover, has it's own motivation.

Categories of Gifts

There are various ways to divide or catalog the gifts. This particular method has brought great joy and understanding to many Christians.

Motivational Gifts

A motivational gift is that _inner drive_ that God gives us in order that we may focus on a particular aspect of Spiritual ministry. Every Christian has one of the 7 motivational gifts listed in Romans 12:6-8 and this gift motivates them to think and act the way they do. We view other _Christians_ and _circumstances_ through our motivational gift.

Ministry Gifts

A ministry gift provides _opportunity_ for recognized Christian service through the church. These gifts are _confirmed_ by church leaders. They include pastor, teacher, church worker, and administrator.

Manifestation Gifts

A manifestation gift is the _supernatural_ result of the Holy Spirit's work in our lives and also in the lives of those to whom we _minister_.

As we _develop_ and _use_ our motivational gift through our given _ministry_, God causes _supernatural_ manifestations to occur.

"Now there are different kinds of gifts, but the same Spirit. And there are different kinds of service, but the same Lord. And there are different kinds of working, but the same God works all of them in all men."
I Corinthians 12:4-6

Here are the gifts broken down into the three lists

You have one *Motivational Gift* Romans 12:3-8	You have one or more *Ministry Gifts* I Cor 12:27-31	You might have many *Manifestation Gifts* I Cor 12:7-11
Prophecy Serving Teaching Exhortation Giving Ruling Mercy	Prophets Teachers Serving (Helps) Ruling (Administration) * apostles * healings * miracles * tongues	Word of wisdom Word of knowledge Faith Discerning of spirits * prophecy (foretelling) * healing * miracles * various tongues * interpretation of tongues

* These gifts are controversial so we're not going to address them in this study. Some believe these gifts are still valid in the church today and some do not

Even though we might have characteristics of many of the gifts because of Christ living in us, we will still be *motivated* by one thing, and that is our motivational gift of which we have only *one*.

However, every Christian can also have one or more *ministry* gifts, and any number of *manifestation* gifts.

The ministry gifts are confirmed through the *church*. The manifestation gifts are determined by *God* through the *Holy Spirit*.

Let me try to illustrate this to help you get a clearer understanding. I have the motivational gift of prophecy (first column). I received this gift at the moment of my salvation and will have it all my life. The motivation of the person with the gift of prophecy is to proclaim God's Word so that others will get what God is saying. This motivates me in everything I do.

I have been involved in three ministries (second column) - the ministry of teaching life group (teaching), the ministry of being a Christian secretary (Serving or helps), and the ministry of speaking before groups of women (prophecy).

Are you with me so far? I have one motivational gift of prophecy, but the Lord has given me 3 ministry gifts of teaching, serving and prophecy. These ministry gifts can change from year to year. My motivational gift never changes.

Now, where do the manifestation gifts fit in? When I am exercising my motivational gift of prophecy through any of the three ministries God has given me, there will be supernatural manifestations (column 3) both in my life and in the lives of those I am ministering to.

For instance, while I am giving my message I might speak a word of wisdom or a word of knowledge or show forth faith in my life. Also the people who are listening to me might manifest some of these things in their lives. One might receive wisdom in dealing with a problem, one might receive knowledge of something that was not quite understood before, or there may be a person who will grow in faith by hearing and believing the Word of God that I speak.

So while I have only one motivational gift which is prophecy, the Lord has given me 3 ministry gifts, and many manifestation gifts.

So let's move on and learn about the motivational gifts from the book of Romans so you can determine what yours is. Discovering this gift will bring you such joy and purpose as you continue your Christian walk.

The Motivational Gift
of Prophecy

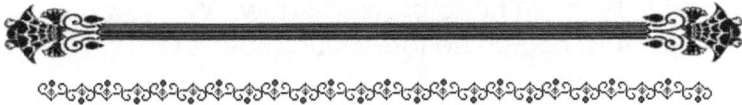

This section on the Motivational gift of Prophecy
Is adapted from "How To Understand Spiritual Gifts", Bill Gothard,
Institute in Basic Life Principles, 1983.

≈ *Prophecy* ≈

Word Picture:
"To shine like a lamp in a dark place"

Shedding light so that you can realize where you are and make wise decisions as to what to do next. Where there is light, there is less stumbling, falling and injuries because you can see where you're going.

In Old Testament times prophecy had two aspects - foretelling and forthtelling.

Foretelling involved direct revelation from God in regard to the future. The Scriptures were not complete at that time, so God gave special revelation to prophets to tell people truth that they could not otherwise know. We now have the complete Word of God so foretelling (special revelation) is no longer necessary.

The other aspect of the gift - forthtelling - was to proclaim the Word of God that man already knew and apply it to everyday situations concerning the times in which they lived. This aspect of prophecy is still carried on today.

Prophecy is one of the most vital gifts given to the Body of Christ. Throughout all the ages, God has called specific people to proclaim His truth to both believers and unbelievers.

I Corinthians 14:3 says, *"But he that prophesies speaks to men for their strengthening, encouragement and comfort."*

I Corinthians 14:23-24 says, *"So when the whole church comes together and everyone speaks in tongues, and some who do not understand or some unbelievers come in, will they not say you are out of your mind? But if you will prophesy when they come in, they will listen and be convicted. As a result, they will fall on their faces, repent and believe."*

Prophecy is the Spirit-given ability to proclaim the written Word of God with clarity and to apply it to contemporary situations.

The Greek word for prophecy is *Propheteia* and it means "To _speak_ before a _group_"

Their motivation: To _proclaim_ the _Word_ of _God_ with _clarity_ and _power_. They want you to get what God is saying!

Remember, motivation is the reason we do the things we do, the reason we feel a certain way, for behaving in a certain manner. The person with the gift of prophecy isn't trying to judge you and condemn you . Their whole motivation is to help you get what God is saying so you won't come under judgment. Everything they say and do stems from this motivation. Out of love, they are trying to warn you.

Their focus: the _message_.
Their whole focal point is "What does God have to say about that?" And they naturally spend a lot of time in God's Word so that they know exactly what God says.

There has never been a time in history that someone hasn't had this gift, because at all times God had someone speaking forth His Word - both men and women. Prophets are like God's loud-speakers strongly proclaiming the Word of God - "LISTEN, THIS IS WHAT GOD SAYS!"

There are many examples of prophets in the Bible - Peter, John the Baptist, Isaiah, Jeremiah, Anna, the four daughters of Philip, just to name a few.

Characteristics of the person with the Gift of Prophecy

1. They have a deep understanding of and belief in the *truths of God*

This seems to mark them from the time they are a new Christian, right up to their maturest point. They understand what God is trying to say and they believe He is telling the truth. "God said it, I believe it, and that settles it."

2. They have the power to make the truth known to others with *clarity* and *conviction*

If you listen to a speaker and at the end you say "Well, I'm not sure of what they were trying to say, but it was a fun time." Then you can be sure that person did not have the gift of prophecy.

The person with the gift of prophecy is message oriented. They want you to get what God is saying. So even if they tell a funny story or use an illustration, it will always be for the purpose of enhancing the message that they want you to receive from God. They have a very definite goal in mind and do not veer from it.

3. They feel compelled to express their thoughts *verbally*, especially regarding *right* and *wrong*

A person with this gift has to speak up regarding sin. They are compelled (motivated) from within to make known God's thoughts on the subject.

With the prophet, there are not very many gray areas. Something is either black or white and God is either for or against it. They cannot overlook sin and worldliness - they must speak out against it and urge people to live holy lives.

4. They possess an amazing ability (discernment) to identify _attitude_, _character_ and _motives_ of other people, and to reject dishonesty in any form

They come on strong because they can discern the consequences of attitude and behavior. They know if you get away with something now, it will be even more of a problem in your life later.

When they detect hypocrisy or insincerity, they will identify it and speak against it. However, the person with this gift must be filled with the Spirit and learn to balance their hatred for sin with love for people.

5. They are open about their own _sin_, _faults_, and _failures_, and want people to point out their blind spots

They keep short accounts of sin. They want holiness to rule and reign in their heart and in the hearts of others. It is their deep heart's desire to be holy.

6. They have a genuine concern for the _reputation_ and _program_ of God

They are sensitive when people blame the church and the work of God. They are defensive for God's reputation and program, and they are willing to suffer in order to defend God's program. They will do what is right in spite of consequences that come from people who are the enemies of God.

7. They have a tendency to be _painfully direct_ when they are confronting someone. They want you to hurry and gets things right so that God won't have to _discipline_ you

They come on strong because of a genuine concern for consequences in your life. Their underlying motive is to get that thing corrected in your life before you really blow it. In other words, they are trying to protect you.

8. They are _persuasive_ in defining what is right and wrong, and strong for appealing for _outward change_

Because of their discernment, they're thinking, "if you say you are correcting this, where is the evidence in your life that you are doing so?"

They look for immediate results in correcting the problem. (The gift of mercy, on the other hand, doesn't expect immediate results, it is more patient. These two gifts balance each other, and we need to learn from the other gifts in order to have a balanced life.)

9. They have a strong _dependence_ on _Scripture_ to validate their convictions

They are motivated to say "here is what God says." They want people to view their correction or discipline as not based on their opinion, but that you know "Thus saith the Lord!"

The right way to discipline is "I see something in your life that you and I need to talk about, and I want to tell you what God says about it." This transfers the authority to God and not the prophet.

10. They have a strong desire to be _loyal_ and _committed_

They will hang in there with you even when you're wrong. In Matthew 26:33 Peter says "Lord, everybody else will leave you, but not me." The prophet doesn't always live up to their sense of loyalty and commitment, but the desire is there down deep in their heart to be a loyal and committed friend and stick with a person.

11. They are willing to experience _brokenness_ in their
    lives in order to see God work in others

The prophet sees the "big picture." They know that God
uses broken vessels more effectively than He does
unbroken vessels. They have the attitude "Whatever it
takes for my will to break, that's what I am willing to do."
They know the value of humility, submission and
brokenness to effectively serve the Lord so that God's
power can be seen in them.

12. They have a tendency to make _quick judgments_

In conversations with Jesus, Peter was the one who usually
spoke up first, or at least got his 2 cents worth in.

How the Person with the Gift of Prophecy is Misunderstood

1. Their strong sense of _right_ and _wrong_ sometimes
   is interpreted as intolerance by others

The prophet sees everything as black and white. No gray
areas. They're not interested in the details which
sometimes leads to "situation ethics." They are only
interested in what God has to say about it.

For example - Abortion. The prophet knows that God says
abortion is murder. It is taking the life of a human being. It
doesn't matter whether the child was conceived in rape,
whether the child is "defective," or whether it's the case of a
choice between the mother's life or the baby's. It is still
abortion. Abortion is still murder. And murder is wrong.

2. Their strong desire to _proclaim_ the _truth_ is
   perceived as disinterest in listening to another
   person's point of view

They know the truth. They see the sin and know where it will lead. Therefore they would like to help you get to your destination safely.

3. Their _frankness_ may be viewed as harshness or insensitivity

They want to immediately get to the root of the problem. No beating around the bush. They see what is wrong and they tell you. They would benefit from learning a certain degree of gentleness when dealing with others.

4. Their interest in _groups_ may be interpreted as disinterest in the individual

The prophet wants to get the word out to as many as possible. They are at their best when speaking before a group, because they can be too intense one-on-one.

5. Their effort to gain _results_ may seem as if they are being too pushy, and some may feel they have a wrong motivation

The prophet sometimes seems to have an "end justifies the means" type attitude.

6. Emphasis on _decisions_ may appear as neglecting spiritual growth

Someone might say to the prophet "You just want someone to make a decision outwardly, you're really not interested in their spiritual growth." But the prophet knows that the first step is getting someone to the point of making a decision, and they want to get that done and behind them, because spiritual growth cannot take place until a definite decision is made.

7. Public _boldness_ and strict _standards_ may hinder personal relationships

Because prophets appear self-confident and self-controlled in their lifestyle, people often reject close friendships with them. Those who are called by God to exercise this gift would like to be accepted and build relationships with others.

The prophet, being misunderstood, must learn to deal with these areas of misunderstanding and call upon God for their strength and comfort.

The key to success for the prophet's life is _humility_. Die to self and let Christ live His life through you. Do not try to do things in your own strength.

How the person with the gift of prophecy behaves when:

Walking in the Spirit	Walking in the flesh
1. Commited to truth	Deceptive
2. Obedient to God	Willful, rebellious (they're going to have their way, no matter what)
3. Sincere	Hypocritical (camouflage their true feelings and manipulate)
4. Virtuous (life and mind is pure)	Sensual (Pray – Lord, take me home before I bring you shame)
5. Bold (their authority is the Word of God, not personal opinion)	Fearful (uncertain and anxious)
6. Forgiving spirit (They get angry, but get over it quickly)	Reject people (not concerned about them)
7. Very persuasive (it is easy to see their point of view)	Argumentative (turns people off)

When walking in the Spirit, the person with the gift of prophecy is effective, persuasive, and fruitful. The enemy, Satan, is going to be doing everything he can to cause them to walk in the flesh so that they will not be effective, and become a problem among the people of God.

A PROPHET EVALUATES ANOTHER
PERSON'S LIFE AND MINISTRY
BY WHETHER THEIR CHARACTER
MATCHES THEIR WORDS.

Ways Women Can Effectively Use their Gift of Prophecy

Speaking before groups of women or children
Teaching/Leading Bible studies
Teaching life group/Sunday school
Teaching new believers
Teaching seminars
Teaching on specific topics
Writing - books, magazine articles, Bible studies,
Sunday school curriculum
Intercessory prayer for those known to be
on the wrong path
Confronting sin (speak the truth in love)
Family life (teaching children right from wrong,
and how to love and follow God)
Christian films - writer, producer, or actress
Book Reviews
Mentor/Discipler

Pat Welch

When I first discovered I had the motivational gift of Prophecy, it was an eye opener. I could never understand why I was so strongly motivated to speak out against sin and injustice. Other Christians I knew were pretty laid back and swept a lot of things under the rug, but I could never do that. When I learned the characteristics of the gift, the light bulb went on, I could see myself clearly, and I understood for the first time why I think and react the way I do regarding people and events.

When I became a Christian at the age of 31, I had a strong desire to study the Bible and apply it's truth to my life. I would spend hours each day digging out the truth of God's Word and developing it into messages. I would then deliver these messages from God first to teenagers and then to women as I spoke in Sunday school classes, Bible studies, seminars, and conferences. I prayed God would make His message clear and powerful through me so that people would get what God was saying and do what He wanted them to do.

Even in making this book available, my motivation is that more women would know the purpose God has for their lives through their spiritual gift and that they would use it for His glory and get great joy out of doing so.

God has had to teach me to hate sin but still love the sinner because the downside of the gift is that sometimes it's hard to separate the two. He placed in my immediate family two mercy gifts which he has used to gentle me over the years. I won't lie, sometimes it has been a painful learning experience, but well worth it as He has balanced out my gift and given me a greater ministry because of it.

There isn't anything that brings me more joy and fulfillment as proclaiming the Word of God to women, and knowing that God has a purpose and plan for my life that far surpasses anything I could have done on my own.

Amy Bush

Like many women who grew up in a Christian home going to church their whole lives, I had heard many sermons on the topic of spiritual gifts. I had studied a variety of compilations of lists taken from various Bible passages.

As I got older I took tests to determine what gift the Lord had given me. Many of these tests ended up being nothing more than a device to determine what I naturally did well. It wasn't until I was involved in one of Pat Welch's Bible studies on the motivational spiritual gifts that I gained any confident clarity in identifying my own. Once I determined that sharing God's truth was my motivation, it became easy to identify that my gift was prophecy (proclaiming truth).

My passion is ignited when I am given an opportunity to share the truths I've found through the study of God's word. It is when I have the most powerful sense of the Holy Spirit working through me and when I have seen Him significantly touch the lives of others through the truths shared.

Pat's teaching took the focus off of my abilities or inabilities and put it on God's awakening and enablement. I will forever be grateful that God used Pat's gift to help me to discover mine.

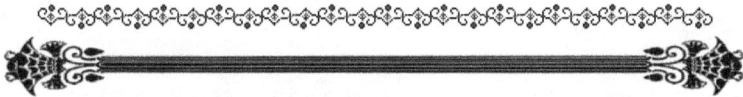

The Motivational Gift
of Serving (Helps)

This section on the Motivational gift of Serving
Is adapted from "How To Understand Spiritual Gifts", Bill Gothard,
Institute in Basic Life Principles, 1983.

≈ Serving (Helps) ≈

Word picture:
"Setting the stage for others"

Serving is the Spirit-given ability to serve joyfully and diligently in a supporting role to help others accomplish their goals.

The Greek word for Serving is *diakonia* and it means <u>helping</u> and <u>supporting</u>. It literally means to take a burden off someone else and place it on yourself. In a church setting, it is the gift that comes alongside leadership so that the leader can concentrate on spiritual priorities.

This gift is quite different from the gift of prophecy because it is ministered faithfully behind the scenes. It is a serving gift, not a speaking gift. There is usually no public recognition, just loving service from the person with the gift.

Their motivation: To meet <u>needs</u> by getting the <u>job</u> done

Their focus: <u>Tasks</u>   (What can I do to ease the burden for someone else?)

Biblical examples of people with the gift of serving are Timothy and Phoebe.

Serving is probably one of the most widespread and needed gifts in the Body of Christ because "Many hands make light work."

Characteristics of the person with the Gift of Serving

1. They have an alertness and sensitivity to practical *needs* and a desire to *meet those needs*

When they're meeting needs, they feel fulfilled, and often do more than is expected. Paul spoke of Timothy serving in Philippians 2:19,20.

2. They receive *joy* in helping others when it *frees* others to do more *important* things

They have an attitude of "I am willing to invest my life in yours to help you be successful." However, they become grieved when they see the person they are serving squandering their time and wasting it on minor things.

3. They have a tendency to disregard personal *health* and *comfort* when serving others

They will forget their health, how they feel, and their own goals, and will give of themselves untiringly. They are willing to work as many hours as needed to get the job done. They need to learn from the person with the gift of Ruling how to delegate in order to work more effectively.

4. They need to be *appreciated* in order to confirm that their service is *necessary* and *satisfactory*

They are willing to give of themselves untiringly, but they need to know they're not wasting their time. When they feel appreciated, they do an even better job next time, and are willing to do even more than they've done in the past.

Every employer would like a group of people who have the gift of serving. The server's contentment lies in the fact that they have done a job and have done it well.

5. They have a strong desire to be with *others* because it provides opportunities to *serve* them

They want to be with people so they can learn about their practical needs, and then they will give of themselves to meet those needs. (This is a great gift for a mother to have).

Oftentimes you find a person with the gift of serving teaching Sunday School. She hears about the need and knows that no one has come forward to meet that need. Finally, she can't stand it any longer, so she volunteers.

6. They like _short-ranged_ projects and become _frustrated_ with long-range responsibilities

This is because their contentment and fulfillment and motivation comes from seeing a project completed. They like to take things "a bite at a time", and if they are given a long-range project, it needs to be broken down into smaller, workable goals.

7. They have a tendency to feel _inadequate_ and _unqualified_ for spiritual leadership

They feel more comfortable behind the scenes, getting the job done for others who have leadership roles.

How the person with the Gift of Serving is misunderstood

1. In their quickness to meet needs, they may appear to be _pushy_

The server jumps to the forefront and says "I'll do it. Don't worry about it." Other people who are listening might think or say "Wow, is she ever pushy!" But the server just wants to get in there and get it done.

2. Their desire to dive in and get the job done may result in _excluding_ others from the job

They're thinking, "if you'll just get out of my way and don't bother me then I will be able to get the job done."

It isn't that they want to exclude everyone. It's just that they see what needs to be done, they know how to do it, and they can get it done faster by not including others.

When a mother or grandmother says "Just stay out of the kitchen, and I'll get the meal on the table," she is really saying "I appreciate your help, but it just slows me down." That being said, servers need to learn to let other people minister to them once in a while.

3. Their disregard for their own _personal_ needs makes them have the tendency to disregard their _family's_ needs too

They need to be appreciated, and they often get more appreciation outside the home than from their own family. When that happens, they might be tempted to put others before family and spend a lot of time helping them. If they continue to put the needs of others before family, they will have major problems down the road.

We hear stories all the time of women who feel they are being "taken for granted" because their family never expresses appreciation for all they do for them. They just expect her to do it and even give her grief if she doesn't perform to their expectations. So finally she decides, well if my family doesn't appreciate me, I know others who will.

The server needs to learn that her family must come first no matter what, and her family needs to let her know that she is appreciated and loved.

4. Their _eagerness_ to serve may prompt suspicion by others of _self-promotion_

Someone might say, "All they want to do is to promote their own cause, and they're willing to step on anybody else to get it done."

The truth is they like to see projects done, and as soon as they finish, their next thought is "What's the next project?"

5. They may _react_ and be _critical_ towards others who are not quick to meet _obvious_ needs

The server is thinking "I wonder what's wrong with these people. Nobody wants to help. All they want to do is talk about it."

6. They are sensitive _emotionally_ when their offer to help is _rejected_

They tend to get hurt and their feelings are very close to the surface. However, they sometimes volunteer to do things they are not good at or are not qualified to do just because they see the need. Then when their offer is rejected, they feel hurt or angry instead of realizing that they just are not qualified in some areas that need a quality job done.

7. Insistance on _serving_ may seen like they are rejecting others who want to serve them

Oftentimes it is difficult to do something for a server because they are already two steps ahead of you. They get "antsy" when they are being served and sometimes you have to say to them "you are depriving me of the joy of serving you."

8. Their desire to sense _sincere_ appreciation may result in their being _hurt_.

When they do their best to serve you and you don't

compliment them and encourage them and reaffirm them, after a while they begin to draw back into their shell.

They act that way because if you don't compliment them, they don't know whether you're pleased with what they have done, and it puts them a little bit out of balance. They don't know what to do next because their desire is to please and help you.

9. Their *quickness* to meet needs may interfere with *spiritual* lessons God is teaching those with the needs

Sometimes God has a person's attention for a purpose and is not ready to meet their need yet. Then the server comes along and wants to meet that need right now! What happens is the server is getting in the way of God's plan, and if they're not careful, they'll be getting pressure from God.

A server needs to ask God for wisdom and discernment so that they don't interfere with God's work in another person's life.

10. They sometimes appear not to be concerned about *spiritual* matters because of meeting practical needs

You may not think they are doing anything spiritual like leading in prayer or teaching a Bible lesson, or spending hours in Bible study. They may even feel they're not as spiritual as others. But what they do is a ministry and extremely important, and we need people who will serve.

In truth, they are doing something spiritual because they're exercising their spiritual gift that God has given to them to minister to the Body of Christ.

11. Their ability to work _quickly_ and for _long hours_ may come across as insensitivity and impatience with others who are _slower_ and get _tired_ more easily

It sometimes seems like people with the gift of serving are like the energizer bunny when everyone else is tired and wants to take a break. They are intent on getting the job done in the shortest period of time because there is a great sense of fulfillment in knowing they did a super job, and they want to speed up that process.

12. Their _enjoyment_ of short-ranged goals may result in _frustration_ and _disorganization_ when given long-range projects

Give them something they can do in a relatively short period of time and they will be highly motivated. They can become discouraged when looking at mountainous projects that take a long time to accomplish.

13. Their inability to _avoid_ the needs of others may sometimes cause problems

When urgencies come up, they get sidetracked. If something appears to be more urgent than the project they're working on, they get sidetracked. Bosses don't like this, and the person with the gift of serving needs to develop balance in her life in this area. They can learn from the Ruler how to set priorities and goals, and to delegate what they don't have time to do.

The server is a "_people person_." However, they need balance if they don't want others to lose respect for them.

How the person with the gift of serving behaves when:

Walking in the Spirit	Walking in the flesh
1. Sensitive and alert to needs	Insensitive – they could care less
2. Hospitable	Lonely – they avoid people
3. Generous with their time	Stingy with their time
4. Joyful when working	Self-pity (pouting) "Why me?"
5. Flexible	Resistant to change
6. Available to meet needs	Self-centered (Why can't someone meet my needs for a change?)
7. Endurance to do whatever needs to be done	Quitter

> A SERVER EVALUATES ANOTHER PERSON'S LIFE AND MINISTRY BY HOW THEY SHOW GRATITUDE, AND IF THEY ARE A HARD WORKER

Ways Women Can Effectively Use Their Gift of Serving

I've listed just a few ways a server can get involved. There are many more as she sees needs. She just needs to make sure she is qualified for whatever she wants to do, or can be trained to do it if she is not.

Secretarial work/Office Help
Meals for people - new moms, invalids, grieving families

37

Cleaning
Fixing things
Doing chores for people
Teacher's aide
Arranging transportation
Setting up chairs
Working in the nursery
Welcoming committee
Arranging flowers/Gardening
Making quilts for nursing home patients
Receptionist
Treasurer
Hospitality
Babysitting/child care
Sewing
Helping at banquets and special events
Food pantry/Food Kitchen
Gift baskets - assembly and delivery
Helping people move
Vacation Bible School
Short term mission trips (helping missionaries)
Writing letters

Carrie Gulbrandson

I believe my motivational spiritual gift is "serving." When I hear that a person has a need, it does my heart good to provide for their need, if at all possible. For example, in one church I attended, if a family needed meals for some reason, I was one of the first ones who would get a call! It was hard for me to say "no"!

For 20 years I was the Administrative Assistant to the Executive Director of a Christian organization. In order for him to be able to travel and minister in the U.S. and abroad, he needed someone in the home office "to take care of business". I praise the Lord for the wisdom He gave to me to represent my boss well.

However I use my spiritual gift, it's because of my abiding relationship with the Vine – Jesus Christ.....John 15:5.

Jane Tedder

At six years of age I trusted Christ as my Savior. As a teenager I was singing in churches, at rallies and in programs. Often people commented that my voice was a gift from God. It was only after studying the gifts of the Spirit that I understood that my singing was a talent with which I was born, not the special gift promised to every believer.

For years I had found joy in anticipating and meeting the needs of others, looking for ways to do things more creatively and efficiently. Whether I was ministering to an individual or a group, I was energized and blessed. It was then I realized that the Holy Spirit had given me the gift to serve. Though this gift can often go unnoticed, the labor, when motivated by love and performed in the strength God provides, produces joyous satisfaction.

As I near eighty years of age I continue to pray for ways to make life easier and more pleasant for others. Using my serving gift is a way to spread the fragrance of Christ in my world and perhaps introduce someone to the greatest Gift of all - the Lord Jesus Christ.

I have worked with patients and families under hospice care. I've visited often in nursing homes and presented weekly programs. I've worked with mentally challenged individuals, and visited incarcerated women on a weekly basis. I've cleaned, organized and done household chores for the ill or disabled.

Currently I am calling three homebound women on a daily basis, taking a sixteen month-old baby for weekly therapy sessions, providing transportation to doctor's appointments for a disabled woman, and meeting weekly with women who have asked to be discipled. Of course, in my role as the wife of a pastor, I have had many opportunities to use my gift and get great satisfaction and joy from it.

Elaine Welch

I discovered my spiritual gift when I took a spiritual gift test back when I *was in high school*. Serving came out on top for me, with teaching and ruling fairly close behind.

When I use my gift of serving, I feel very fulfilled. God uses me to see needs within the church and to help meet those needs. I'm the person who is happy as a clam working in the background. You can find me in the kitchen serving food, cleaning up, and generally doing the tasks that need to be done so that the other gifts can be free to do what God has enabled them to do. I am always drawn to the service type roles in any church I have been in.

There have been times, due to personal circumstances, that I've "sat in the back row" and not gotten involved in the church for a period of time. When I have done this, there has been no joy because I'm not serving. I think of Lumiere in "Beauty and the Beast" – the song when he sings about "how sad is the servant who isn't serving."

One thing I have discovered is that serving needs to be balanced because a pitfall of this gift is getting over-involved and over-committed. Being sensitive to God's leading in using any gift is important.

The Motivational Gift
of Teaching

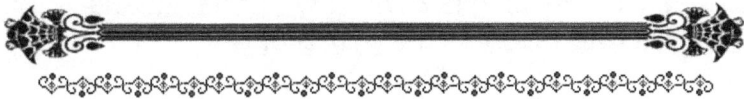

This section on the Motivational gift of Teaching
Is adapted from "How To Understand Spiritual Gifts", Bill Gothard,
Institute in Basic Life Principles, 1983.

≈ *Teaching* ≈

Word Picture:
"Turning on a light so you can see"

After you have heard a teacher teach, your response should be "I see what they mean." The light goes on!

Teaching is the Spirit-given ability to study and communicate truth effectively so that people can learn.

You should not confuse the natural talent with the spiritual gift. We should never assume that one is spiritually qualified to teach Sunday school because she is a public school teacher.

The Greek for teaching is *didaskalos*, and it means <u>systematically</u> teaching the <u>*Word*</u> of <u>*God*</u>.

Their motivation: To <u>*convey*</u> God's <u>*exact truth*</u>

Their focus: In-depth <u>*study*</u> of <u>*God's Word*</u>

Biblical examples of people with the gift of teaching are Luke, Priscilla and Aquila.

Luke 1:1-4 shows that Luke clearly had the motivation of a teacher:

"...since I myself have *carefully investigated everything from the beginning*, it seemed good also to me to write an *orderly account* for you...so that you may know the *certainty* of the things you have been taught."

Luke did not treat the Word of God lightly, or just believe what someone else had told him. After he heard or read something, he would investigate it for himself to see if it was true.

Characteristics of the person with the Gift of Teaching

1. They have a desire to present truth systematically, so it can be clearly _understood_ and that others can _learn_

The information they convey can be followed easily and we can almost know what will come next. They usually have a subject, a theme, and use an outline form.

2. They place great emphasis on the _importance_ and _accuracy_ of words

"What did you really mean by that?" "Is that the most accurate word to describe what the Bible is saying?"

They are sticklers for words and shades of meaning. Sometimes they can become irritating in the fact that they want you to prove everything you are saying by the Word of God.

3. They have a delight in _researching_ and _recording_ as many facts on a subject as possible

For example, Luke wanted to give a "detailed" account. The teacher spends a great deal of time digging and researching and going back and checking resources and validating all the facts. Then they share - not just the surface information, but layer after layer of detail.

4. They have a God-given interest in _details_ not noticed or mentioned by others

They're not satisfied with just the general idea, but need to know every detail. The prophet wants the message; the teacher wants the details.

5. They have the tendency to test the _knowledge_ and _credentials_ of those speaking or teaching

"Tell me about that. How did you arrive at that conclusion? Where did you get your information? Are you sure it's validated? Are those statistics really accurate?"

It's not that they're nosy or hard to get along with, but they have a genuine interest because that's the way God wired them.

It's very important that God places within the Body of Christ many people who have the gift of teaching because it keeps our theology and doctrine clean and pure.

The teacher is geared to accuracy and thoroughness in research and making sure that what is said is absolutely the truth. This helps in discerning error from truth within the Body of Christ.

6. They have a greater joy in _researching_ truth than in _presenting_ it

They love to spend time discovering the truth - delving into this knowledge, checking that shade of meaning. They are a spiritual "Sherlock Holmes," always investigating and looking for clues that lead to truth.

They are often satisfied even if they never formally tell anyone else. They have gained and acquired knowledge and therein lies their satisfaction.

7. They tend to avoid the use of _illustrations_ from non-_Biblical_ sources

No tear-jerking stories - just stick with the Word of God. They have a tendency to be a little narrow in this area, not understanding or realizing that sometimes an illustration simply enlightens our mind for deeper understanding of spiritual truth. They could learn from the prophet or exhorter in this area.

8. They have a tendency to remain *silent* until information has been *heard* and *discussed.* They are not *impulsive*, but slow and deliberate

They listen, they think through it, they observe, they calculate. Only then do they make a statement, and when they do speak, they appear to be far more authoritative.

9. They have a tendency to *validate* new truth by running it through established systems of truth, based on the *Word of God*

When they investigate carefully, they compare what they already know to be true against what they are hearing now. Everything has to be sifted through what has already been established. And that is very good! We can all learn from the teacher.

How the person with the Gift of Teaching is misunderstood

1. The emphasis on accuracy of Scriptural information may appear to neglect *practical application*

The teacher needs to remember to make the truth effective in the lives of others, rather than just gathering facts and having head knowledge. They can learn from the prophet and the exhorter in this regard. It's great to have knowledge, but we must apply it to our lives.

2. Vast knowledge may make the teacher appear to be *proud*

The teacher's great love for learning is a gift from the Lord, therefore there is no room for pride. It's not the teacher, but the Holy Spirit who enlightens people's minds. The teacher needs to be careful that they are filled with the Spirit and maintain an attitude of humility.

3. They may tend to be _critical_ when they spot small, factual errors in the teaching of others

The teacher needs to be careful not to be critical if someone is not quite as informed as they are.

4. Their desire to impart details of research may appear to their listeners as _boring_ and _unnecessary_

The teacher wants others to appreciate their research which they have spent so much time on, but they have to remember to keep in mind other people's ability to comprehend and retain new material.

5. Their emphasis on _research_ by studying what other people have written may make them appear to be dependent on others rather than on personal study in the _Word of God_

The teacher, like all the other gifts, needs balance. They need to go to the Word of God each day not just to study, but for a personal message. "Lord, speak to my heart today. Open my eyes, that I may behold wondrous things out of Your Word. Excite my heart and cause me to worship you." The prophet can teach them in this regard.

6. Their emphasis on _research_ may appear as though they despise the _practical wisdom_ of less educated teachers

Degrees behind the name do not guarantee wisdom, wise decision-making, or skill in communication. Some of the wisest people in the world do not have a Master's degree.

They are simply students of the Word of God.

7. Their need to be _objective_ in research may make
    them appear to be _unfeeling_ and _cold_ when
    teaching

The teacher needs to learn to see people and how God's
Word can speak to their needs. This will make their
teaching so much more effective.

How the person with the gift of teaching behaves when:

Walking in the Spirit	Walking in the flesh
1. Self-contolled	Self-indulgent
2. Reverence for God's Word	Treats God's Word like a textbook
3. Diligent in study	Lazy
4. Thorough	Leaves things dangling
5. Dependable	Inconsistent
6. Secure in God	Anxious
7. Patient	Restless

I hope you have noticed by now that when you walk in the
flesh, you get the exact opposite result of walking in the
Spirit.

If we are not filled with the Spirit when exercising our
spiritual gift, it doesn't matter how good we are.   It will
make no eternal difference, and will be burnt up as "wood,
hay and stubble" at the Judgment Seat of Christ.
(I Corinthians 3:12-15)

> A TEACHER EVALUATES ANOTHER
> PERSON'S LIFE AND MINISTRY
> BY HOW ACCURATE THEIR WORDS
> ARE WHEN THEY SPEAK OR WRITE.

Ways Women Can Effectively Use Their Gift of Teaching

Sunday School/Life Group teacher
Home Bible study teacher
Vacation Bible School teacher
Teaching Seminars
Children at home - teaching object lessons
Christian school teacher
Teaching a college class or elective
Mentoring
Writing Bible study or Sunday school curriculum
Research and word studies
Teaching doctrine to new believers and/or
church members
Children's ministry
Book reviews
Editing
Church library - organizing, maintaining, updating,
gathering new books and resources

Testimony Time - Gift of Teaching

Bonnie DiBlasi

There is a chorus that says "He brought me to his banqueting table, His banner over me is love," and that is the truth of my life. Every morning, very early before the day breaks, God meets me, coffee cup in hand, at my kitchen table, and there is spread for me His banqueting table of love! My kitty cat "Sassy" shares the time.

It's all about His Word. The table is spread with commentaries, dictionaries, maps and Bibles. This is no casual thing – these tools are always there because I go back throughout my day and night to see what new truth God has for me!

I have been digging out the little gems, the research, and recording layer after layer of truth! – even to the checking out of other's teaching and preaching of the Word of God, always using the Bible and some old established works on the subject.

I rarely teach someone else's material; it's best for me fresh from His Word, and empowered by the Holy Spirit then and there.

At my study table, sometimes with a pot of spaghetti sauce on the stove, I text Bible verses to my grandchildren every day, and even other family members. It is in this place I pray for them, and where I share my deepest self with God and go from strength to strength in His Word.

Although it is rare when I use other people's material, I have especially enjoyed and used Pat Welch's teaching on "Spiritual Gifts" and often refer to it in my Bible studies – especially if I am teaching about a person of the Bible. It is always such a delight for me and my students.
In my life it's all about the Word of God and the teaching of that word in the power of the Holy Spirit as I trust Him to fall fresh on me!

My husband drives me faithfully to and from my Bible study and also faithfully prays for me as I seek to study and share God's Word. He has always done this and I am blessed!

Armed with God's Word, the power of the Holy Spirit, a faithful church and pastor, a praying husband, I have to ask . . . How good is that?!!!

Many times I have felt physically unable to teach, but I go with His promise of II Corinthians 12:9,10, and He has brought me through.

"My grace is sufficient for you;
for my strength is made perfect in weakness."
II Corinthians 12:9a

Pam Marshall

I grew up attending Sunday school and could give detailed accounts of the more renowned Bible stories. I even won prizes for Scripture memory. In my teenage years when I came to know Jesus as my Savior, I felt compelled, almost immediately, to know more about the Bible. At that time, however, I didn't recognize this desire as a spiritual gift.

Over time, the Lord directed me to churches and people where Bible study was valued as a tool for Christian growth. In one of these studies, I discovered the spiritual gifts. Since every believer has at least one, I determined to find mine. I listened to messages, read books and looked at various descriptions of each gift. I also examined the Scriptures and cross-referenced various passages, yet God used a conversation with my pastor's wife to clarify everything for me. Her question, "What brings you the most joy in your Christian life?" made me think. I quickly responded with "Studying the Word of God and learning." She then told me that was a good indication my gift was teaching.

I decided I would give teaching a try and started as a 5th grade Sunday school teacher. Later I taught Jr. Church and ladies Bible studies. When teaching children, especially my own, I often used object lessons. Once we were weeding in the garden, and I pulled out an onion. I used it to illustrate how very many layers were present and how each one moved you closer towards the core. In the same way, the Word of God is like a book with many layers. We can read and study the same verses, and each time we do, God reveals more of Himself to us. It is like peeling that onion. There is still more to come.

I still love discovering the details of God's plan through the ages in both

50

the Old and New Testaments. I take courage from learning how He worked in the lives of everyday people to bless and develop a relationship with them. And best of all, I gain strength and wisdom from verses that speak directly to me in my life situation at any given point.

One of my greatest joys is to study a verse or passage of Scripture and sense God teaching me. The joy continues when I share it with others and then watch the light go on as they get excited about the Word of God. One thing I try to do is to make my presentations interactive -- with object lessons, role plays and group projects. My desire is that the people in my classes discover the truth for themselves as opposed to using a lecture method, and I've seen good results. This way of teaching fits with the person God created me to be and generates profitable discussion as participants make their own discoveries in truth.

I find that I must rely on the Holy Spirit to transform my words to impact others for His honor and glory, and I get truly excited to hear that something He taught me also blesses them.

The Motivational Gift
of Exhortation

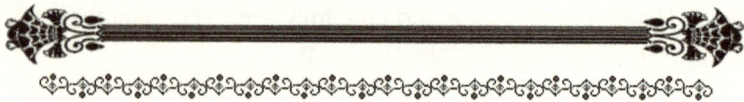

This section on the Motivational gift of Exhortation
Is adapted from "How To Understand Spiritual Gifts", Bill Gothard,
Institute in Basic Life Principles, 1983.

≈ *Exhortation* ≈

Word picture:
"Stepping into your life to light the fuse of growth."

Exhortation is the Spirit-given ability to help another by motivating them to action.

The Greek word for exhortation is *para; kaleo*. This is the same word used in John 16:7 when it speaks of the Holy Spirit. It means one who is called to walk alongside to <u>encourage</u> and <u>comfort</u>.

The exhorter accepts us just the way we are, yet is able to see the potential in our lives and encourage us to meet that potential. Think of the exhorter as cheering you on to spiritual growth.

Their motivation: To cause <u>*growth*</u> in <u>*people*</u>

Colossians 1:28,29 speaks of the heart of Paul's motivation for ministry:

"Whom we preach, warning every man and teaching every man in all wisdom, *that we may present every man perfect in Christ Jesus.* For this I also labor, striving according to His working, which works in me mightily."

Their Focus: Steps of <u>*action*</u> to help people <u>*grow*</u>

The exhorter compliments the work of the teacher. The teacher brings us to say "I see that." The exhorter brings us to say "I'll do that." Teaching is directed to the learner, while exhortation is directed to those who have knowledge and need to know how to apply it to their lives.

Biblical examples of people with the gift of exhortation are Paul and Barnabas.

Characteristics of the person with the Gift of Exhortation

1. They urge others to full _spiritual maturity_ in Christ

The exhorter wants to know where you are in your spiritual walk, and what you're doing to promote growth. They're not interested so much in activity, but in attitudes. "What is God doing in your heart?" They want you to take deliberate steps in order to grow.

2. They have the ability to visualize the _"Big picture"_ of what you're capable of accomplishing and becoming spiritually

They want God to use them to help you become the person God wants you to be. They're thinking of what you can do if God had all of your life and you were totally surrendered to Him. They can see your potential.

3. They have _insight_ into where you are _spiritually_, and take you on from there

They usually start asking questions. "Where are you in your relationship with God? What is God doing in your life?" They are extremely anxious for spiritual growth in your life and want to see the fruit.

4. They give you precise _steps_ of _action_ to take you from where you are now to where God wants you to be

Exhorters make good counselors. "Let me walk with you and help you get on the right path."

It is one thing to be told you are doing wrong. It's another thing to be told "Here are the steps to follow to have victory over that problem." The teacher is satisfied teaching truth, but the exhorter says, "What good is the truth if you're not going to help them grow by giving them steps to apply it to their lives!"

5. They tend to welcome personal _tribulation_ because they know it produces _spiritual growth_

The exhorter is willing to suffer because they have learned the value of suffering, the value of discovering God in their trial. They see tribulation as a tool in the hand of God to make you more like Christ.

Their attitude during trials and suffering is "Learn God's lesson and move on to the next step."

6. They have a tendency to avoid information that lacks _application_

For example, when a speaker is speaking, the teacher is asking "Is what she says accurate? The prophet wants to know the message from God. The exhorter is thinking, "Is she going to tell us how to do what she just told us we should do? If not, then what good is it?"

7. They desire _face_ to _face_ discussions to ensure a _positive_ response

They read your facial expressions and your body language when they are talking to you, because they want to see if you're hearing, receiving, believing and applying what they are telling you. The exhorter is grieved when you tune them out. They want to help you discern where you are, why you got there, and how to come out of that into victory. They're not interested in small talk.

8. They have an ability to discover *insights* from personal *experience* which can be validated and amplified in Scripture

The teacher or prophet goes first to the Word of God and then makes an application from their study. The exhorter watches your life, then goes to the Word of God to find the principles they can take back to you to help you personally grow.

9. They are motivated to bring *harmony* among diverse groups of believers

They do well in the midst of disputes because they see it as a challenge. They will work with both sides and encourage growth and unity.

10. They enjoy being with people who want to *learn* and *grow*

They love to minister to people who might not be doing what is right but have the desire to do right and are willing to listen.

11. They usually are not involved with people on the basis of a *long-term* commitment

When they get you on the right path and they see that you're growing, they look around for the next person to help. It's not that they're not interested in you anymore, but someone else needs their help more. They get their greatest joy from helping others get back on track.

How the person with the Gift of Exhortation is misunderstood

1. Their steps (1-2-3) of action may appear to oversimplify the _problem_

They know those simple steps come straight from God's Word and can give genuine deliverance if followed.

2. They may appear to be _over-confident_ in giving counsel and advice

Again . . . they know God's principles work, so they have a sense of urgency when they tell you about it.

3. Because their primary interest is in _growth_ and _discipleship_, they may be perceived as having a lack of interest in personal _evangelism_

God gives a different emphasis to different people, and all the gifts together make a beautiful balanced fellowship and family of God.

One of the best ways an exhorter can use their gift is to come alongside a new Christian and teach them how to walk and to grow into a mature Christian. This is so needed in the church today.

4. Because of their great desire to make Scripture _practical_, some people may think they take it out of _context_

And sometimes the exhorter is tempted to do just that. They need to learn from the gift of teaching to be more accurate in their Bible study and make sure what the Word of God is saying in a particular passage.

5. They may seem to disregard the _feelings_ of others because they put so much emphasis on _steps_ of _action_, and they know _tribulation_ is good for you

You might be thinking "They really don't care about me and what I'm going through. They don't care about my feelings."

The exhorter knows that you are going to grow through the trial, and to them it is worth whatever suffering you will go through.

How the person with the gift of exhortation behaves when:

Walking in the Spirit	Walking in the flesh
1. Wisdom	Self-effort
2. Discernment	Judgmental
3. Faith in God	Confidence in self
4. Discretion	Simple minded
5. Unconditional love	Selfish
6. Creativity	Laid back
7. Enthusiasm	Apathetic (could care less)

The exhorter is a beautifully equipped person who encourages other people to grow. When walking in the Spirit, they are a dynamic motivator to the glory of God.

Every believer would do well to have a personal friend who is an exhorter to help keep them on track and motivate them to do better.

The person with the gift of exhortation needs to patiently Instruct from the Word of God (II Timothy 4:2). At the same time, they must realize that some people will respond almost immediately to what they are saying, while others will ignore them, try their patience, and refuse their advice.

> AN EXHORTER EVALUATES ANOTHER
> PERSON'S LIFE AND MINISTRY BY WHETHER
> OR NOT THEY SHOW PEOPLE HOW TO DO WHAT
> THEY HAVE TOLD THEM THEY SHOULD DO, OR
> JUST LEAVE THEM "HANGING"

Ways Women Can Effectively Use Their Gift of Exhortation

Seminar speaker
Teacher for life group/Sunday school
Speaker for ladies conferences/Retreats
Coming alongside new Christians
Counseling women, teens and children
Discipling/mentoring
Writing
Music
Family life
VBS teacher
Crisis Center
Hotline Help
Hospital visitation
Home visitation - newcomers, elderly, sick, grieving
Welcoming committee
Letter writing

Testimony Time – Gift of Exhortation

Ellen Garland

There is a spiritual intrigue about finding one's spiritual gift. The intensity for me to personally find mine was vital. As an adult, it was one of the boosts in my practical walk with God; and as a young adult, it helped me not to compare myself with others, but to realize that I was unique.

At age 22 I had the joy of sitting under Pat Welch's teaching on Spiritual Gifts. The practicality of learning the traits of each gift, the Biblical basis, as well as how they fleshed out, gripped my heart. Though it was years ago, the path of exhortation was clearly marked, and "ready or not" I began to travel on it.

Based on the Spirit of God, it has been the joy of my heart to consider where a person is at (Point A) and where they can get to (Point C), but motivate them along the path (Point B). Side by side, shoulder by shoulder, heart to heart, life is about growth with that single word, "together" becoming my focused frame.

Today I live out my spiritual gift, based on my purpose statement, "Igniting others to skillfully apply truth." I have found opportunity to live it with my soul-mate, as a mom, discipling young ladies, even in the Wal-Mart line! I am with Word of Life local church ministries, a youth coach, and Genreal conference speaker for girls who want to know genuine and for women who want to impart real. Thank you, Pat, I am indebted to your teaching.

Cathy Mara

I remember sitting in a fabulous Sunday school class and listening intently to Pat Welch teaching on spiritual gifts. Pat took her time going through each gift in detail stating both the positive and negative aspects of each gift. When she started teaching on the motivational gift of exhortation, I became more and more excited about all that I was hearing. I found that both the positive and negative aspects of the gift truly fit me to a "T", and I knew I was an exhorter through and through! My desire to encourage people finally had a name – Exhortation. Even before I recommitted my life to the Lord, I found myself building others up.

From that lesson came a career change. For the next few years, I focused my attentions on sales, and sales management. I was also a corporate trainer. I love public speaking and encouraging others to meet their sales goals. I also enjoyed training so much! To be able to train, encourage and help others achieve their sales quotas was very rewarding.

The Lord started tugging on my heart to take my spiritual gift even further and my life became very interesting! Pat's husband had gone back to school and graduated from Trinity College with his Bachelor's degree, and he encouraged me to go forward in my education. I'm so glad I did! Now armed with a degree and knowing what my real calling was, I decided to leave a very high paying job to work in social services, namely, Big Brothers Big Sisters. That job, and those following, totally have utilized my spiritual gift of exhortation.

I am currently a licensed Mental Health Counselor and work as a licensed assessor for BayCare (The Harbor). I also have a part-time private practice that I am trying to build up. Every single day I am using the knowledge that God has seen fit to give me. Every client I counsel, no matter who they are, leave my office knowing they are cared for and encouraged. I consider it an honor to be able to serve in this capacity.

My private practice is also very rewarding. In this venue I am able to provide Christian counseling, and being able to counsel with a Biblical approach is so meaningful.

The Motivational Gift
of Giving

This section on the Motivational Gift of Giving
Is adapted from "How To Understand Spiritual Gifts", Bill Gothard,
Institute in Basic Life Principles, 1983.

≈ Giving ≈

Word Picture:
"Prospering to enhance God's work"

Giving is the Spirit-given ability to be sensitive to and contribute material resources to the needs of the saints with joy and generosity.

This gift is not reserved for the wealthy. The issue is not the amount of the gift, but the ability to give abundantly out of whatever you have.

The Greek word for giving is *Metadidomi*, and it means "*to super-give*"

The giver does not give to impress people, or because they feel it is their duty. They have a strong desire to give as much as they can to glorify God.

Their motivation: They *live* to *give* so that God's *work* will be *produced*

Their focus: *financial needs*

Biblical examples of people with the gift of giving: Matthew and Lydia

Characteristics of the person with the Gift of Giving

1. They have an ability to make wise *purchases* and *investments* in order to have money available to *give away*

Because they live to give, they're always very careful about how they spend their money. They don't usually waste it on frivilous things for themselves or others.

2. They desire to give *quietly* to effective projects and ministries without *publicity*

They are not motivated by applause and prominence. They get satisfaction and fulfillment just by the act of giving. They are not looking for public approval.

3. They enjoy meeting needs without being *pressured* to give

The person with the gift of giving is motivated from within by God to give, not from outward pressure. They are turned off by high pressure tactics.

4. They have a desire to use their giving as a way to *motivate* others to give

They envision what can be accomplished if everyone pitches in and gives what they can. They see the possibilities and envision the end result.

Malachi 3:10
"Bring all the tithes into the storehouse,
that there may be food in my house.
Test me in this, says the Lord Almighty,
and see if I will not throw open the floodgates of heaven
and pour out so much blessing that you will not
have room enough for it."

They know the value of giving - that as we give we receive a blessing. They want you to get into that cycle so they try to motivate others to give by being an example in their own giving. Not just money, although that is their major focus, but they will give of their time and whatever else is necessary to make an impact for God.

5. They have the ability to see _financial needs_ that others tend to _overlook_

They seek ways and means whereby God can use them to give.

6. They have the ability to discern people's _wisdom_ and _faithfulness_ by the way they handle funds

Luke 16:10,11
"Whoever can be trusted with very little can also be trusted with much, and whoever is dishonest with very little will also be dishonest with much. So if you have not been trustworthy in handling worldly wealth, who will trust you with true riches."

It's not money that is bad - it's the love of money that is bad. We all know people in the public eye who have been caught embezzling or using money inappropriately. This is especially sad when it is a Christian. The person who is entrusted with large funds has an awesome responsibility before God to be a good steward.

7. They have a tendency to be _frugal_ and content with the _basics_ (necessities of life)

They don't need to be surrounded by things. They desire an uncomplicated life.

Their motivation isn't great wealth in order to extend their own resources. Their motivation is to accumulate as much as possible so that they can give it away as the Lord leads.

8. They have great _joy_ when a gift they give is an answer to _specific prayer_

No matter how much they give, they have joy because God

used them to answer prayer. It confirms to them that God is in this and that they understood when God spoke to their heart.

They don't thrive on the compliments of the person that they give to, but in their heart they are saying "Lord, thank you that you entrusted me to give, and help me to always be sensitive to what you tell me so that I will be right on target with my giving." This is what rejoices their hearts.

9. There is a dependency on their _partner_ to confirm the _amount_ of the gift

When there are two believers who are partners (husband/wife or business partners), the giver strives for unity before they give. They believe that God will show both partners the same thing. This may take some time because we are not all at the same stage of spiritual growth, and in some cases we have read God wrong, and our partner will keep us from giving indiscriminately. The giver needs to be patient and pray that if God wants them to give, then in His timing He will put that on the partner's heart as well.

10. They have a concern that their gift be of _high quality_

Their gift represents the intensity of their desire to be a good steward before the Lord in what they're giving. Their gift also represents them. It is a gift worthy of their love and their caring. "Here is how I feel in the value of my gift."

11. They desire to be a part of the _work_ (ministry) of the person to whom they _give_

They don't want to control or dominate, but they want to be

a part because they are giving in obedience to God. They love to give, and they want to see God accomplish His purpose.

How the person with the Gift of Giving is misunderstood

1. Their need to often deal with large amounts of _money_ may appear that they focus on _temporal_ values

Because they have the gift of giving and feel responsible for large sums of money (or even small amounts), they want to be very careful of where it goes and how it is being used. They want to be able to give a good report to God on their stewardship.

They may appear to be temporal minded when that's not the case at all. They just feel responsible to God for the sums of money He has placed at their disposal.

2. Some may think they want to _control_ or _dominate_ a ministry by "buying" power or authority

A person with the gift of giving who is walking in the Spirit would never do this. They don't manipulate, they just humbly give.

3. Their attempt to get others to _give_ may seem to be "_putting pressure_" on people who have less to give

Their intention is not to put pressure on you. They just want to encourage you to get in on the blessing. (Read Deut. 15:7-10)

4. Their lack of response to "_personal appeals_" may appear as a lack of generosity

If they are listening to God, they don't need the pressure of people asking them for money. It tends to make them back off and withdraw because they are very cautious and careful.

Pressure urges them for a quick response, so they react by backing off which makes them appear selfish and uncaring.

5. Their *personal* frugality may appear as *selfishness* in not meeting the "wants" of their family and friends

They are always thinking, visualizing, planning ahead and saving up to meet the needs that God shows to them. Therefore, when their family wants some kind of a luxury, the person with the gift of giving is not always eager to provide for that luxury because they don't want to waste God's money.

The person with the gift of giving has a tremendous opportunity to be a blessing to God and people. They also have a tremendous opportunity to motivate the rest of us who don't have that gift, and encourage us in the work that God has called to do.

How the person with the gift of giving behaves when:

Walking in the Spirit	Walking in the flesh
1. Thrifty	Extravagant
2. Resourceful	Wasteful
3. Content	Coveteous
4. Punctual (on target)	Tardy (lets chances go by)
5. Tolerant	Prejudiced (not wanting to give to a particular person or group)
6. Cautious	Rash (gives indiscriminately)
7. Thankful	Unthankful

A GIVER EVALUATES ANOTHER PERSON'S LIFE
AND MINISTRY BY THE WAY THEY INVEST THEIR
LIVES, POSSESSIONS AND TIME. IS IT
WORTHWHILE, AND DOES IT HAVE ETERNAL
VALUE?

Ways Women Can Effectively Use Their Gift of Giving

The woman with the gift of giving may use it to meet needs wherever she finds them. If she is married, she must be sure to have unity with her husband on this matter, and not just go and do things on her own.

*Scholarships - Christian schools, camp,
Short-term missions
Short-term mission trip leader
Child evangelism
Teach workshop/seminar on finances or
money management to adults,
and teens
Missions ministry - writing letters, monthly
support of missionaries, meeting
personal needs of missionaries
Vacation Bible School - helping with games,
crafts, refreshments
Food pantry - giving and working
Placing Bibles - Gideons
Bus ministry
Special events - decorating, setting up,
participating*

Testimony Time - Gift of Giving

Sharon Hughes

My motivational gift is giving. One of my former pastors taught on gifts and that is how I found out what mine was. I have never even thought about not tithing, giving to the needs of the church, or people. I love putting food in the church food pantry. God has always provided for us and I have never felt any downside to giving. I've heard people say "Can you imagine what we could buy if we didn't tithe," but my thought is "Can you imagine the blessings we would miss out on if we didn't."

I remember a time when our former music minister's car was in the shop and he didn't know how he was going to pay for it. We didn't know that at the time, but the Lord laid it upon our hearts to send him a check. It was enough to cover the repair and he said it was an answer to prayer.

I can't say which I love more, giving or evangelizing. I love to hand out tracts or just start a conversation with someone and eventually lead them into a conversation about the church or the Lord.

Dorothy Salen

I first learned about giving from my Mother. During the depression even if we didn't have money to keep the gas on, my mother always tithed to the church and gave money or food where needed.

A lot of my grandchildren are mission minded and the Lord always nudges me to give toward their missions trips. Sometimes I have a certain amount in mind, and the Lord tells me to give more or less than I planned on giving. I follow what He tells me.

Other ways I give is for kids to go to camp. One time some little boy who couldn't afford to go otherwise wrote me a wonderful note. I also give to missionaries and Jericho Rd. Ministries. My son has a rehab house called the Jesus Inn, which I also give to. I enjoy giving! I thank the Lord for that gift.

70

Sarah L.

Even before I came to know the Lord, I was a giver because my family taught us to think of others and their needs. Not just gifts of money, but other resources, and helping others as well. Once I accepted Christ as my Savior, the giving and helping continued in different areas – God's people and Christian organizations at the top of the list.

I learned early on in my Christian life that one cannot outgive God. If there is a need . . . help! If there is something to be done . . . do it! Money may not return as money but perhaps the vehicle will last another year or the roof may last longer.

Being a very practical person, and concerned about how I spend the money God allows me to have, I look for bargains at yard sales and consignment shops for myself so that I can have more money to give to the needs of others that God shows me. I have found God to be faithful through 60 years of following Him, and continue to see His hand of mercy each day.

The Motivational Gift
of Ruling

This section on the Motivational gift of Ruling
Is adapted from "How To Understand Spiritual Gifts", Bill Gothard,
Institute in Basic Life Principles, 1983.

≈ *Ruling* ≈

Word Picture:
"Piloting a ship safely to port"

Ruling is the Spirit-given ability which enables someone to clearly understand both immediate and long-range goals, and to organize and mobilize people to reach those goals.

The Greek word for ruling is *kubernesis* and it means <u>*to steer a ship*</u>

Their motivation: To put the <u>*pieces*</u> together to form the <u>*"big picture"*</u>

Their focus: <u>*The completed project*</u>

The ruler knows how to form objectives to reach a goal and they know how to mobilize people to get the goal completed.

Two words define the gift of leadership: <u>*direction*</u> and <u>*decision-making*</u>. A true leader is like a shipmaster in the storm. When the going gets rough, they keep the ship on course and everybody reaches the destination. The ruler has the ability to keep the ship on course during the storm.

Biblical examples of people with the gift of ruling: Nehemiah, Jethro, Titus

Along with the gift of Prophecy, Ruling is the most misunderstood of all the gifts because of their responsibility, and sometimes because of the way they come across. They are "take charge" type of people.

Characteristics of the person with the Gift of Ruling

1. They can see the "*big picture*" and visualize the final results of a major undertaking

They picture the project already accomplished and completed, and know the key to completion is goal-setting! They have a sense of direction because they have a picture of the finished project in their heads.

2. They can break down large goals into *smaller achieveable* tasks

They are never discouraged by the size of a task because they know that all things are possible in bite-size pieces. We could all take a lesson from this.

3. They are *self-starters*

When you show them the goal, they want to get on with getting the job done. Their motivation for starting is so that they can begin to watch the parts of the project fall into place.

4. They have the ability to know what *resources* are available and needed to reach a *goal*

When they see the goal, they are sensitive to what is available to get the job done: people, money, time, knowledge, equipment, ability, talent, gifts.

The ruler does not need any negativity - they need to think positively of the way to reach the goal. And God is looking for positive people who are willing to believe and trust in His resources.

5. They know what can and cannot be _delegated_

They know how to find people to do what they don't know how to do. They don't try to take everything on themselves. The server could learn a lot in this area from the ruler.

6. They have a tendency to remove themselves from the little details in order to focus on the "_ultimate goals_"

In accomplishing anything, someone has to keep the big picture in mind. Someone has to be sure that we're all headed in the right direction and that all the parts are fitting into one whole. The ruler cannot afford to get bogged down in all the little mundane things behind the scenes - that is why they delegate and supervise.

7. They are willing to endure other people's _negative_ reactions to their plan

The person with the gift of ruling must have "tough skin." The Ruler stands out in front and gets most of the flack. It's part of the responsibility of management. If they allow themselves to listen to the negative thoughts of others, they will never continue to move forward. The person with this gift cannot afford to be super-sensitive and take everything personally. They can't be a "people pleaser!"

8. They need to know that the people they are leading have _confidence_ in them and are _loyal_

Because they are loyal, they expect loyalty from others. When they find disloyalty, they are grieved in their heart. They can become very upset because the goal is in danger of not being accomplished if there is disloyalty in the ranks.

9. They will assume the _leadership_ position if no structured leadership exists

The person with the gift of ruling waits, and if nobody else rises to take responsibility, they will move forward and say "I'm willing to assume leadership if necessary." They don't usually run to the front, but sit back and see if anybody else takes charge. But they can only wait for so long before they have to get in there and get things together.

10. They have a desire to _complete_ the _project_ as soon as possible

They do not get their joy from people's applause and praise, but in the satisfaction of seeing all the parts come together to complete the big picture.

11. They have great _joy_ and _fulfillment_ when all the parts have come together and others are enjoying the _finished project_

Their attitude is to accomplish this as orderly as possible, as well as possible, and as quickly as possible. They are conscious of time, quality and stewardship.

All of us should live ordered lives and can learn great lessons from the person with this gift.

12. When the job is complete, they move on to a _new challenge_ (What's next?)

When the ruler has gone about tackling the project systematically, and then sees it accomplished, they will start thinking about the next project. That's the way to keep things moving and progressing.

How the person with the Gift of Ruling is misunderstood

1. They may appear _lazy_ because they _delegate_ work

If a person is a good manager, they are not going to try to do it all. They are going to try to involve as many people as possible and necessary to bring all the resources together to get the job done.

2. Their willingness to endure the _negative_ reactions of others may sometimes make them appear to be _callous_

Again, the person has to have a "tough skin" because you can't please everyone. They cannot afford to be sensitive to criticism.

3. Because they view people as _resources_, it may make people think that they are being "_used_"

Instead of complaining, our attitude should be "I'd be happy for the Lord to use me in any way possible if it would bring glory to Him and help to accomplish His work here on earth."

4. They may give the impression that _projects_ are more important to them than _people_

It's not that people aren't important to them, but their focus and motivation is to see all the parts come together to form the big picture. This is what brings them joy. They know that people are important because God uses people to accomplish His work. They usually give credit to everyone involved in getting the work accomplished after it is done.

5. The desire to complete the project _quickly_ may make them appear to be insensitive to the _schedule_, _priorities_, and _weariness_ of others

"I'm tired. You don't care about how I feel." To the ruler the question is not how you feel, but is the objective worthy of the sweat, blood and tears of getting the job done?

They have the attitude "Lord, whatever it takes, I am willing to give of myself." We should never settle for less than our God-given capacity.

"Whatever your hand finds to do, do it with all your might." Ecclesiastes 9:10

How the person with the gift of ruling behaves when:

Walking in the Spirit	*Walking in the flesh*
1. Orderly (organized in their thinking)	Disorganized
2. Has initiative (self starter)	Apathetic
3. Responsible	Unreliable
4. Humble (motivating people out of loyalty, not intimidation)	Proud (intimidates others; dogmatic, dictator, turns people off)
5. Decisive (strikes while the iron is hot)	Double-minded
6. Determined (goal is worthy of the price)	Fainthearted at obstacles
7. Loyal	Unfaithful

A RULER EVALUATES ANOTHER PERSON'S LIFE AND MINISTRY BY HOW LOYAL THEY ARE TO THE PERSON FOR WHOM THEY WORK, AND IF THEY FAITHFULLY FOLLOW THROUGH ON THE RESPONSIBILITIES THEY TAKE ON

Ways Women Can Effectively Use Their Gift of Ruling

Directing Vacation Bible School
Supervising an office
Sunday school /Christian Education Director
Organizing a fund-raising event
Women's Missionary Fellowship leader
Women's Ministry Leader
Organizing meals and transportation
Organizing their home and delegating responsibilities
to their children to help them learn to work
Organizing socials for life groups or church
Planning a Ladies Conference
Church administrator
Committee chairperson
Missions coordinator
Music ministry leader
Nursery coordinator
Workshop or seminar leader
Organize mission trips
Teach workshop/seminar on organizational skills

Testimony Time – Gift of Ruling

Fay Phillips

As I think over my life, I am very thankful that God revealed to me at an early time that I have the gift of Ruling (Administration). I was only in my twenties when God opened up the opportunity in California to administrate a fairly good sized preschool at the church we were a part of.

It didn't seem like I really searched for my spiritual gift . . . the Lord just put me in circumstances where I walked through the doors he opened for me. I was always motivated and excited to minister in that role.

As time went by, I found mself on the brink of another "new" administration position in the Word of Life ministry in Florida. This was a ministry that really reached into the lives of women and encouraged them in their different areas of need. Our ladies conferences challenged me, and being able to orchestrate well-known women on a national level to minister to the women who were in my area of ministry was very exciting and rewarding. I enjoyed delegating the work amongst our staff from planning the menus to printing the programs and everything inbetween. I remember being very exhausted at the end of these conferences, and yet very exhilarated at the thought of being able to be used in that capacity by my precious Lord.

I guess if I were to give any advice on how to use your gift, it would be to always keep an open mind and a willing heart to do whatever God brings into your life. It is very rewarding.

Judy Revere

As an adult Christian I knew about spiritual gifts but never was real curious about them until one Sunday morning something the minister said caught my attention. He had been systematically going through the gifts and I always thought I knew mine. I liked teaching and I was successful at it, therefore I had always assumed my gift was teaching.

However, as the pastor mentioned the gift of administration I felt something stirring inside. Each trait he mentioned about administration seemed to be something I liked doing in the church. I had been the Sunday school superintendent for years, I spoke in youth groups about colleges and college prep, ran the summer D.V.B.S. program and organized parties to honor different church members for their service. So I began to think . . . and to pray.

The pastor had said that if you weren't sure of your spiritual gift you should ask a good friend or your pastor, so that's what I decided to do. Can you imagine my surprise when my best friend just looked at me and said that my gift was in organizing and administration! I went to my pastor as well and he immediately told me my gift was administration. That's when I had the "AHA" moment.

Now, many years later I trust God to help me use my motivational spiritual gift, but I also like to use other gifts as I am able. It has been a great learning experience.

Nancy Patterson

I have always had a head for business. Wherever I worked, I became a leader, even if my position didn't require it. When I started working as church treasurer, it just seemed natural for people to come to me with any questions or issues that needed to be addressed.

After a few years, I was offered the job as Business Administrator at the church. It was my dream job, but I hesitated. At the time, my husband and I had a business, and I helped him. I was concerned that I wouldn't be there for my husband, but I was more concerned that I was not equipped to do what the church needed. I didn't want to let God down so I did not accept the position. After a couple of weeks of no peace, I prayed again. My husband told me that I needed to take the job, because as he stated, "it is your passion." At that time it was so clear that I needed to do it for God. I approached the church and they gave me the job.

A few months later, I decided to take a spiritual gift test, and the test revealed that my spiritual gift was Ruler (administrator). I am thankful that God "pestered" me and didn't let me miss out on this incredible blessing.

Sometimes those of us with the gift of Ruling may not be as warm as we need to be. I feel compassion and mercy, but sometimes when people are sharing with me, I automatically go into problem solving mode. Instead of just listening with a merciful ear, I want to help them fix things, and may give unwanted advice. I know that at times people may perceive that as uncaring, and it hurts me that I may come across that way. God is helping me to use my spiritual gift by opening doors, and also teaching me and giving me the wisdom necessary in using it well.

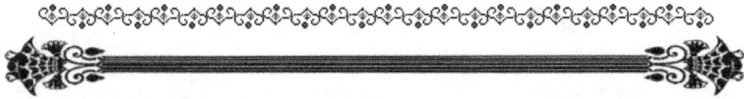

The Motivational Gift
of Mercy

This section on the Motivational Gift of Mercy
Is adapted from "How To Understand Spiritual Gifts", Bill Gothard,
Institute in Basic Life Principles, 1983.

≈ Mercy ≈

Word Picture:
"A sunbeam to the suffering"

One author wrote "Showing mercy sparkles like a diamond against a dark background of indifference."

Mercy is the Spirit-given ability to feel compassion for and minister joyfully to those who have physical, mental and emotional problems.

The emphasis here is on the word *joyfully*. A pleasing countenance in acts of mercy is a great relief and comfort to those in misery when they see that mercy is not given grudgingly and unwillingly, but with pleasant looks and gentle words.

Cheerfulness is so important with this gift because they are usually dealing with the sick, distraught and grieving individual, which reflects depression, rather than joy. Mercy comes in with a quiet cheerfulness that comes from the heart and expresses itself in smiles, patience, kindness and songs.

The Greek word for mercy is *eleon*, and it means *pity, mercy*, and *compassion*

Their motivation: *To heal the hurt*
> They want to get inside and help people who are hurting.

Their focus: *Hurting people*

Biblical examples of people with the gift of mercy: John, Dorcas (Tabitha), the good Samaritan

Mercy is not a feminine gift - mercy is a characteristic of the Lord Jesus Christ. It is a character quality that God wants all of us to express and experience, so we must learn from the person with this gift, just as they need to learn things from us in order to balance their gift.

The person with the gift of mercy must be tough on the one hand, but very tender on the other. They are the joy of the Body of Christ. They equalize and balance off some things that people with the other gifts would miss.

Characteristics of the person with the Gift of Mercy

1. They are *sensitive* and can discern the *feelings* of others. They know when to *speak* and when to be *quiet*

God has granted to them a level of sensitivity whereby they can approach a group, a family or an individual, and discern the feeling level of where people are emotionally. They can determine whether there is joy or sadness behind the smile. This is very basic to how God uses the gift of mercy because they operate so often on a feeling level.

2. They have a tendency to be drawn to and understand people who are having *mental* and *emotional* distress

They have a tenderness, openness and willingness to vicariously suffer with them, and the person in this type of distress senses that in their spirit and draws near to mercy.

They have the capacity to weep with those who are hurting, and we all need someone to hurt with us at times. They are God's gift of joy and cheerfulness to the Body of Christ because they can go through the hurt with us, yet maintain their joy and cheerfulness.

3. They want to remove _hurts_ and bring _healing_ to others, rather than allowing others to _learn_ from their hurts

The gift of exhortation says "Let them hurt because it is vital to their growth." Mercy and exhortation can really clash! Mercy needs to understand that God uses hurt and suffering in a person's life in order to bring them to the end of themselves and complete surrender to God.

4. They have a greater concern for _mental_ or _emotional_ distress than for the physical distress of others

They are concerned about the inner sorrow, hurts, frustrations and anxieties. The speaking gifts reach out with words. The gift of mercy reaches out with genuine love and caring that is uplifting, soothing and healing in a time of hurt.

5. They are sensitive to _words_ and _actions_ that will hurt others and come quickly to their defense

If you say something critical and harsh about someone within the hearing of a person with the gift of mercy, everything in mercy tenses up because they are so sensitive to other people's needs and hurts.

Oftentimes the gift of mercy hurts immediately when something of a critical nature is said about someone else. They live with a radar sensitivity. They know how they hurt (and they can be easily hurt), so they know how other people feel.

If they are walking in the flesh instead of the Spirit, they can come back rather harsh and try to set us in our place instead of gently teaching us about being kind to others.

6. They have a tendency to react *harshly* when intimate friends are rejected

They are very, very loyal. When they see or hear of one of their friends being rejected, it's difficult for them, and they're going to react harshly because of their loyalty and faithfulness . They can instantaneously project themselves into that person's situation. They feel the rejection and they quickly respond.

God has placed the mercy gifts into the family of God to help balance other people's responses and reactions to people. Mercy teaches us to think before speaking. Is it kind? Is it necessary?

7. They have an ability to sense *genuine* love, and they have a greater vulnerability to experience *deeper* and more *frequent* hurts because of *lack of love* from others

They are hurt easily. Someone might hurt the gift of mercy and prophecy would say to mercy, "Don't worry about it - it's their problem!" But mercy finds that hard because they are injured deeply and grieving in their heart.

They give and give and give of themselves and they are more vulnerable because they're sensitive to other people's needs. They are hurt on a deep level, and that is why they feel so deeply for others.

The gift of mercy needs to have a mate who is protective, supportive and loving

8. They have a need for _friendships_ and
   commitments on a deep abiding level

Because they deeply give of themselves, they need people
who will participate in a mutual commitment. Again, very
important when choosing a mate!

9. They measure acceptance by _physical_ closeness
   and _quality_ time together

Mercy needs closeness, intimacy, and a genuine
expression of love, or they will suffer on a deep level. They
need their emotional and spiritual cup renewed. Again, very
important in choosing a mate. They need to depend on the
Lord for that right person, not on their own emotions.

10. They have great _unity_ with friends who are
    sensitive to the needs and feelings of others

They are not attracted to critics. They may still choose to
be your friend, but they don't like the way you act when you
are criticizing and judging.

11. They have a tendency to avoid _firmness_ until it is
    absolutely necessary

Because they want to help, and because they hurt when
someone else is hurting, they have a tendency not to want
to express firmness in a situation which may demand
firmness. They need to see that hurting and pain is
sometimes a part of God's plan for that person's life.

It's very important that Mercy understands that there is a
correct time to express their mercy, not right at the crucial
point when God has that person hurting to where they are
just about to give up in absolute desperation and turn
towards God.

Sometimes the most difficult thing in the world is to back off and let someone we love dearly hurt until they can't hurt any longer. But we mature through hurt and we cannot protect people from hurt as much as we might like to.

It's difficult for Mercy to stand back and watch God work His gift of grace in somebody's life. However, they need to learn to do that and to ask God for wisdom in exercising their gift so that they do not interfere with God's plan.

   12. They close their _spirit_ to those who are insincere or insensitive with others

Mercy need to realize that sometimes instead of harshly closing the door on that type of a person, that they have a responsibility to gently and lovingly, by example, teach that type of person to love others.

   13. Their _kindness_ comes naturally

Their very first inclination is to be kind to others. Where most people have to learn kindness, the gift of mercy's kindness comes naturally.

How the person with the Gift of Mercy is misunderstood

   1. They appear to operate on _emotion_ rather than logic

This is because the person with the gift of mercy is motivated to get on the inside and help the person who is hurting. They need to learn to balance their feelings on the Word of God. They can learn much from the speaking gifts in this area.

   2. Their avoidance of _firmness_ may make them appear to be _weak_ and _indecisive_

The prophet, teacher, and exhorter are very firm and rush in. The person with the gift of mercy very gently, very lovingly and carefully moves in to create a healing atmosphere by their words, by their presence, by their touch.

When we are going through a trial, or we are grieving, or when we are entangled by sin, we need the gift of mercy in our lives. But at some point we need firmness also so that we can turn ourselves around and start going in the right direction.

3. They appear to take up other people's _offenses_ because of their sensitivity to _words_ and _actions_ which cause hurt

When they're out of fellowship with God, that is exactly what they do. Maybe someone has been critical toward a friend of theirs. They take up their friend's offense to the point where they themselves are acting unkind and harsh to the person who criticized their friend. In not lovingly dealing with the one who is criticizing, they in turn can become very critical themselves. They need to recognize this and learn to deal with it in their lives.

4. Their ability to detect insincere _motives_ may cause some to feel they are hard to get to know

Some people who are insincere, back off from the gift of mercy because they know that mercy is going to detect that in them. To a sincere person, mercy is the joy of the church and they are easy to get to know.

5. Because they are drawn to and understand those in distress, this may be misinterpreted by those of the _opposite sex_

An example would be a guy who is on drugs, and along comes a sweet Christian girl with the gift of mercy. He shares with her that he feels rejected, hurt, disappointed, discouraged.

Mercy knows that Christ is the answer and reaches down and says "I'll be happy to help you out of that." Mercy doesn't realize the danger that if she keeps reaching down further and further to where the addicted person is, that both of them could become trapped by the same sin. The guy is enjoying her mercy and acceptance of him and would like her to join him where he is.

People with the gift of mercy must be very, very careful that they don't get down on the level of the person they're trying to help to the point where they can't help them. Many people with the gift of mercy have wound up on drugs, alcohol, and in sexual and abusive situations and unequally yoked marriages because they haven't realized the danger and have not depended on God for discernment, nor sought counsel from mature Christians.

Mercy must learn to meet the need, but not become emotionally involved with the other person to the point of forsaking God's laws. It would be a good rule most of the time for the person with the gift of mercy to work mainly with their own sex.

Mercy must be balanced with _wisdom_ and _discernment_ from the Word of God in order to have maximum effectiveness! Otherwise she might begin to think that her gift trumps all others and be prideful. "I'm the only one that understands; no one else seems to care; what is the matter with these people." Mercy has to learn that all the gifts are needed and given by God to minister to and through the church. Mercy needs to be balanced as much as all the other gifts need to be balanced. One gift is not better than the other. They are all important and each one manifests an aspect of God's character.

How the person with the gift of mercy behaves when:

Walking in the Spirit	Walking in the flesh
1. Attentive to hurts of others	Unconcerned
2. Sensitive	Callous
3. Fair	Partial/prejudiced
4. Compassionate	Indifferent
5. Gentle	Harsh
6. Respectful	Rude
7. Meek (humble)	Angry

A MERCY PERSON EVALUATES ANOTHER PERSON'S LIFE AND MINISTRY BY HOW SENSITIVE THEY ARE TO THE NEEDS AND FEELINGS OF OTHERS

Ways Women Can Effectively Use Their Gift of Mercy

Mercy is a personal ministry to

The hungry
Drug abusers
The bereaved
Anxious people
Poor people
Heartbroken people
Orphans
The abused
Unwed mothers
The elderly

Alcoholics
The lonely
The sick
The depressed
Widows
Handicapped
Mentally retarded
Prisoners
Homosexuals

Specific ministries could include:
Food pantry - working, meeting people, counseling
Home visitation
Hospital visitation
Nursing home visitation
Prison ministry
Rescue mission work
Alcohol or drug abuse counseling
Crisis center counseling
Counseling new believers
Homeless shelter
Nursery worker
Deaf ministry
Handicapped ministry
Hospitality
Writing
Vacation Bible School worker
Missionary housing or meals
Women's pregnancy center

Nikala Zentkovich

As a child I was always told that I had the gift of serving. At the age of 20 or 21 I realized I had the gift of mercy and that my motivation behind what I do was geared toward hurting people instead of events. My heart desired to serve children, foster kids, single moms, etc.

Having the gift of mercy has its upsides and downsides. One of the upsides is that I was allowed to help people that others could not because of my desire to just listen and love on them.

One of the downsides for me was that I felt merciful towards so many people, it was easy for me to become depressed. I would see all the needs, and knowing I was unable to fix all the needs was very depressing for me. Another downside was that because I desire to help, many people would take advantage of me and walk all over me until I was at the point of not wanting to do ministry anymore.

Getting married to my "prophet" husband is one of the best things that ever happened to me. Not only because I got to marry my best friend, but because God gave me this man to protect me. His gift is the complete opposite of mine, but it compliments mine perfectly. In fact, my gift has become stronger because I don't feel like I have to be shy or hide from people out of fear of being taken advantage of.

Gail Barnes

I discovered my motivational gift of mercy in a class that Pat Welch taught at our church. Before that I used my gift naturally, not knowing what it was or how to use it to the fullest.

One of the ministries I really loved was going to the Women's prison. As a wife of a Gideon we were allowed to go and do the program for Sunday morning services. The women were always glad to see us and we would bring Bibles to hand out. I also took devotionals that they would share with each other. These women didn't need to be told they were sinners because they knew what they did wrong and why they were in prison. What a joy to be able to give the Word of God to these women and see them saved! I loved going and listening to them sing. They had a choir that sometimes had music and sometimes they sang acappella. The joy and feeling that they sang with was sometimes overwhelming. I always left there filled with joy and knowing that I had been in the presence of the Lord.

I love helping people and my mercy comes into play there. I've been involved when the church supplies food and gifts for families in need. I remember one Christmas a family came to pick up their food basket with their children, and as we were putting the groceries in the car the little girl grabbed an orange and took a bite out of it peel and all. Juice was running down her face, hands and arms, and all she could say was mmm mmmm. It broke my heart to know that they didn't get fresh fruits and vegetables.

I have a business of cleaning houses, and because of my gift, I end up helping these people in times of need. The last couple I was working for, I became their Power of attorney. I took care of the husband and had to put his wife in a home. We would go see her every day, then I would make sure the house and bills were taken care of. He passed away so I moved her closer to my home, set up a trust, and took care of her. She has since passed away, but I feel God had me in their lives to help them emotionally. They had no family here.

I have incorporated many of the gifts in my life over the years, but my natural tendencies go back to mercy.

Jodie Sewall

I was 22 years old when I first heard Pat Welch teach a study on Spiritual gifts at a Bible study at Word of Life. I recognized at that time I had been given the motivational gift of mercy. This gift draws me to the emotional and spiritual needs of others. I seem to be quick to sense when someone is feeling down or not comfortable in a situation. It's as if God has equipped me with a spiritual antenna that receives signals when there is an emotional or spiritual need nearby. It is often perceived by others as 'kindness' – they see that I have come alongside to try and help them in some way.

I am not necessarily drawn to people in physical pain or distress. The truth is I hate to see people suffering physically. If I cannot help remove their pain, then I would rather not be anywhere near as it hurts me to watch them suffer. However when I see emotional or spiritual pain, I can draw near because I know the Spirit of God who dwells within me can meet them in their need and help bring relief.

I am aware of a few areas I can get in the way of the work that God is trying to accomplish through me with my gift of mercy:

- Because I hate to hurt anyone's feelings, whenever I am asked to help someone do something I almost always say yes and often end up with way too much to do. I need to seek God's direction for things I commit myself to and learn to trust that when I say 'no', God will supply someone else to meet their need. This is hard to do.
- I really hate confrontation so I often just sweep the hurts or offenses under the rug and hope they go away. Usually this is just a short-term solution as the bulge in the rug grows too large to ignore. When that happens and I finally let all of my hurt feelings out, they can seem out of proportion to the current issue. This often leads to misunderstanding by others as they think I am making a "big deal" out of nothing, when in fact many things have grown to a big deal. I need to be willing to speak the truth in love, even when it may cause temporary distress in someone's life.
- Because I hate to watch someone suffer, I am not good at letting consequences run their course. I feel sorry for the person who is experiencing the negative consequences and want to rescue them. When I do this, I may be in danger of hindering the transformation work God is trying to do in their life

I need to ask God for wisdom every day in exercising this gift of compassion. I want to have sensitive ears to God's leading so that I can use my gift effectively.

I always assumed that my spiritual gift was serving. I was saved at the age of 11 and started serving the Lord soon after in Youth group, and assistant teacher in my local church. I helped start a bus ministry and did regular visitation with the bus captain.

Later on my husband and I were working at the Word of Life Family Campground in upstate NY. I attended a ladies morning Bible study where the gifts of the spirit were being taught by Pat Welch. Although I was quite certain my gift was serving I thought it would be helpful to discover how all the other gifts worked. As we progressed through the list I was stunned and frankly relieved to discover that my Motivational gift was mercy. You see, I had always felt that something was wrong with me. There were many times I was moved to tears over various events and could not "control" the emotion that would pour out of me. My heart would literally ache over the problems and distress of others that they would share, or I would weep over a song that deeply touched my heart while others around me seemed totally unmoved. So there was relief to realize that it was a gift that had been given to me by God, and I was "normal" in the feelings that were so deeply embedded in me.

Although the gift of mercy brings me joy as I come alongside and help other people through their hurts, there is also a flip side to Mercy. This can be a very painful gift, and sometimes I would love to swap it out and spend the rest of my life developing another gift that would be "more fun." If that sounds unspiritual, you probably don't have this gift and don't understand the deep responsibility that comes with it.

My husband is a pastor and there have been numerous times when I have been torn apart by people who attempt to harm the pastor and split the church. There were some ladies who I thought were dear friends and close to me who later on walked out of my life after trying to destroy my ministry. These are times when I feel ready to quit my ministry and let "others" do the work.

Part of my ministry was to help my husband with counseling sessions with married couples. Many a harsh wife who had no intention of reconciling with her husband stood and screamed at me because of the

"Biblical mandate" to work on forgiveness. We counsel parents who need help in how to deal with their children but will not "do" what is necessary to train them, and I can see the train wreck down the road because of their unwillingness to listen. This is hard to watch with this "gift" of mercy.

I carry many burdens for others that they are not even aware of, and sometimes have sleepless nights praying for "issues" and concerns. Sometimes I want to turn off the feelings that come with this gift and just be "normal" but I know that God has given this gift to me personally and I do want to exercise it as He intended. Most of the time I am thankful for my special gift.

Recently I was blessed when a church member told me that I am the arms of Jesus and shine out His love whenever she encounters me. She said I draw people in with my smile and personal warmth and I'm easy to approach. She said I lead by example in what to do for others and how to follow Jesus. She considers me a burst of sunshine and joy and said I am like a person who braids and weaves and criss-cross others with my life and availability. Even though she knows that there has been hurt and pain caused by others and sometimes even myself....she says I still offer my love endlessly and openly show the love of Jesus. To her I am tireless and energetic when serving the Lord and show love and teach others with joy and example. And I didn't even pay her to say all that! ☺

That was so good to hear and to know that Jesus shows Himself through my gift even when I don't feel it or see it. And it gives me the courage to continue on the path Jesus has laid out for me.

Wrapping it Up

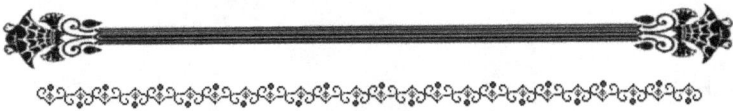

Romans 12 - Motivational Gifts

Gift	Motivation	Focus
Prophecy	To proclaim the Word of God	Message
Serving	To meet needs	Tasks
Teaching	To convey truth	In-depth study
Exhortation	To help people grow in maturity	Steps of Action
Giving	Living to give	Needs
Ruling	Putting the pieces together to form the big picture	The completed project
Mercy	To heal the hurt	Hurting people

All Christians are Generally Commanded by God to:

Prophesy

"Follow the way of love and eagerly desire spiritual gifts, especially the gift of prophecy. . . he who prophesies edifies the church." I Corinthians 14:1,4

Serve

". . . Serve one another in love." Galatians 5:13c

Teach

"Let the Word of Christ dwell in you richly as you teach and admonish one another with all wisdom . . ." Colossians 3:16

Exhort

"But exhort (encourage) one another daily. . .so that none of you may be hardened by sin's deceitfulness." Hebrews 3:13

Give

"Give, and it will be given to you. . ." Luke 6:38a

Rule

"Diligent hands shall rule..." Proverbs 12:24a

Show Mercy

". . .Clothe yourself with mercy (compassion), kindness, humility, gentleness and patience." Colossians 3:12

We can develop all of the gifts in our lives to some extent, when we learn from others who are gifted in areas that we are not.

If one with the gift of prophecy does not learn from a person with the gift of mercy, they may speak the truth, but probably not in love as we are commanded to do.

If one with the gift of exhortation does not learn from a person with the gift of teaching, they may give steps of action for Spiritual growth, but they may not be Scripturally accurate.

If one with the gift of mercy doesn't learn from the prophet and exhorter, they might ignore sin and not give lasting help to the people they minister to.

God gives all the gifts to the church so that we can minister to one another and maintain "balance."

Understanding the basic motivation of each gift:

If all the seven motivational gifts were represented in a family and someone dropped the dessert on the floor, here is what each one might say, and why they would say it.

Mercy — "Don't feel badly. It could have happened to anyone." (Motivation: to relieve embarrassment)

Ruler — "Ann, would you get the mop. Sue, please help pick it up, and Mary, help me fix another dessert." (Motivation: to achieve the immediate goal of the group)

Giver — "I'll be happy to buy a new dessert." (Motivation: to give to meet a tangible need)

Exhorter — "Next time, let's serve the dessert with the meal." (Motivation: to prepare for the future)

Teacher — "The reason that it fell is that it was too heavy on one side." (Motivation: To discover why it happened)

Server — "Oh, let me help you clean it up." (Motivation: to meet a need)

Prophet — "That's what happens when you're not careful." (Motivation: to correct the problem)

How To Understand Spiritual Gifts" Bill Gothard, Institute in Basic Life Principles, 1983, page 29

Understanding how each gift responds to a situation:

If seven Christians who represented each of the motivational gifts visited a sick person in the hospital, here is what each one might say, based on the perspective of their gift.

Mercy   "I can't begin to tell you how I felt when I learned you were sick. How do you feel now?"

Ruler   "Don't worry about a thing. I've assigned your job to four others in the office."

Giver   "Do you have insurance to cover this kind of Illness?"

Exhorter   "How can we use what you're learning here to help others in the future?"

Teacher   "I did some research on your illness, and I believe I can explain what's happening."

Server   "Here's a little gift! Now, I brought your mail in, fed your dog, watered your plants, and washed your dishes."

Prophet   "What is God trying to say to you through this illness? Is there some sin you haven't confessed yet?"

How To Understand Spiritual Gifts" Bill Gothard, Institute in Basic Life Principles, 1983, page 31

What we need in our church

If seven people representing each of the motivational gifts met to organize an ideal church, here is what each one would probably emphasize.

Prophet   Well-prepared sermons exposing sin, proclaiming righteousness, and warning of judgment to come.

Giver   Generous programs of financial assistance to missionaries and other ministries.

Ruler   Smooth-running organization throughout the church so that every phase will be carried out decently and in order.

Mercy   Special outreach and concern for the precise and varying feelings of individuals, with a readiness to meet their needs.

Exhorter   Personal counselling and encouragement for every member to assist them in applying Scriptural principles to their daily living

Teacher   In-depth Bible studies with special emphasis on the precise meaning of words.

Server   Practical assistance to every member of the church to encourage them and to help them fulfill their responsibilities.

Bill Gothard, Institute in Basic Youth Conflicts, 1981

Keeping Our Gift In Perspective

In order not to think of ourselves more highly than we ought to think, and to help us to esteem others better than ourselves, we need to know that:

<u>EVERY</u> Christian has at least one spiritual gift.

<u>EVERY</u> member of the church has a place of ministry.

<u>EVERY</u> member of the Body of Christ needs every other member of the Body of Christ.

<u>EVERY</u> gift is important.

<u>EVERY</u> gift is to be exercised in humility, unity and love. Otherwise it has no value.

When exercised in the Spirit, the gifts should all fit together smoothly and harmoniously. We need to be good stewards of the gifts and talents God gives to us.

When we glorify God, our potential becomes a living reality. God can take the the smallest and the least and the biggest and the most, and make something beautiful out of them.

Your ability grows as you put your gift to work. It's like a muscle - neglect it and it becomes weak and flabby. Use it and it will perform better and better.

Problems in Discovering Your Gift

Some Christians have difficulty discovering their gift even when they read the characteristics and understand the material.

New Christians

A new Christian is busy learning the basics of the Christian faith in order to grow and mature. They might not be ready to discover and exercise their gift yet.

Mature Christians

Christians who have been walking with the Lord for a number of years and have been developing the character of Christ, and learning from the other Christians around them, are to a certain extent developing all the characteristics of the gifts in their lives. They might get a little confused when they try to pinpoint just what their motivational gift is.

They need to go back to their motivation. Why do they do the things they do? think the way they think? react in a certain way? Which gift holds their motivation? What gives them the most joy?

Troubled Christians

A person who has had great trauma in their lives, especially when they were a child, and has not dealt with the past, will have problems discovering their spiritual gift, mainly because they are living in the past.

Uninvolved Christians

There are some Christians who have not been very involved in a local church or ministry for one reason or another. They need to try ministry in different areas and see what they are good at, along with asking God to pinpoint their specific gift for them - the one that will bring them great joy.

Jesus – Our Perfect Example!

Jesus Christ is a picture of each of these gifts lived out perfectly. He was the absolute fulfillment of each one, all at the same time.

As a Prophet:
- He spoke only what He heard the Father speak – John 12:49
- He was the Truth – John 14:6
- He saw into people's hearts – John 4:18
- He prayed and interceded – Mark 1:35
- He hated evil – Matthew 21:13
- He was frank and outspoken – Matthew 23:27

As a Server:
- He worked with His hands as a carpenter with Joseph – Luke 2:51
- He demonstrated service – John 13:5
- He exalted serving – Mark 10:43
- He had a high energy level and kept pace with the demands of His ministry – Mark 10:1

As a Teacher:
- He taught God's truth – Matthew 13:31
- He quoted Scripture – Matthew 4:4
- He built on Scriptural truth – Matthew 5:21-22
- He was intelligent and curious – Luke 2:46
- He was self-controlled – Luke 23:9

As an Exhorter:
- He taught people to live victoriously – Matthew 5-7
- He gave positive exhortations – Luke 6:27-35
- He prescribed precise steps of action – John 8:11; Matthew 19:21
- He accepted people as they were – John 4:4-30; Mark 2:13-16
- His own life was a witness to the truth – John 18:37

As a Giver:

- He fed the five thousand – Mark 6:41
- He gave His time, energy, abilities and love to others – The Gospels
- He taught on giving – Mark 12:42-43
- He had a strong focus on the Gospel – Luke 4:43
- He gave His life for us – John 15:13

As a Ruler:

- He organized His followers – Mark 3:13-14; 9:2; Luke 10:1
- He was highly motivated to fulfill His mission – Hebrews 12:2
- He was under authority and taught about authority – Matthew 28:18
- He was an effective leader – Matthew 10:5-8
- He endured criticism for the long-range goal of the cross – Matthew 20:28

As a Mercy person:

- He had a tremendous capacity to show love – Matthew 14:14
- He was aware of people's physical needs – Matthew 15:32
- He was alert to emotional and psychological needs – Matthew 9:36
- He cared for children – Matthew 19:14
- He had empathy for others – Luke 7:13
- He expressed emotion – John 11:35
- He mourned over Jerusalem – Matthew 23:37

Perhaps no better words can be spoken to conclude a study of Spiritual gifts than those written in I Peter 4:10,11.

"God has given each of you some special abilities; be sure to use them to help each other, passing on to others God's many kinds of blessings. Are you called to preach? Then preach as though God Himself were preaching through you. Are you called to help others? Do it with all the strength and energy which God supplies so that God will be glorified through Jesus Christ. To Him be glory and power forever and ever. Amen."

(The Living Bible)

Get Involved©
by Pat Welch

"I'm too old," or "I'm too young"
We often hear people say
"I've done my part, don't even start . . .
Maybe some other day!"

"I'm retired"; "I'm not qualified"
Are excuses we abuse
When all God wants is a willing heart
In a woman He can use.

The ministries are plentiful
And include both big and small.
But sometimes we just close our eyes
And ignore God's gentle call.

He gives us gifts and talents
To use in ministry for Him.
But sometimes we forget that
And our spiritual sight grows dim.

Soon we'll stand before His throne
To give an account of our life.
How we fared on earth with the roles we played
As friend and mother and wife.

But that won't be all we answer for
When before Him we'll humbly stand
What of the gifts and talents He gave
To minister in the land?

Will He look upon you with sorrowful face
As you realize how much you are flawed?
You lived your life with excuses
And forgot that He was God.

Don't wait until then to do what is good
For then it will be too late.
He's given you what you need right now
And today is a brand new slate.

So whether you're young or whether you're old
Or somewhere in-between,
Get busy doing whatever God says
Wherever a need is seen.

Minister here and minister there,
Whatever you can do.
Your life will be filled with blessings
From letting God work through you.

Bibliography

How To Understand Spiritual Gifts, Bill Gothard, Institute in Basic Life Principles, 1983

Institute in Basic Youth Conflicts, 1981, Bill Gothard

Spiritual Gifts by John MacArthur, Moody Press

19 Gifts of the Spirit by Leslie B. Flynn, Victor Books, 1974

Discover Your Spiritual Gift and Use It by Rick Yohn, Tyndale House, 1974

The Dynamics of Spiritual Gifts by William McRae, Zondervan

You and Your Spiritual Gifts by Kenneth O. Gangel, Moody Press, 1975

Discover Your God-given Gifts by Don & Katie Fortune, Chosen Books, 1987

He Gave Gifts by Chuck Swindoll, Word Publishing, 1992

Unwrap Your Spiritual Gifts by Kenneth O. Gangel, Victor Books, 1983

Other Source Material:
Strong's Exhaustive Concordance, Riverside Crusade Bible Publishers, Inc.